END OF TRACK

By James H. Kyner

as told to Hawthorne Daniel

With an introduction by

James C. Olson

A Bison Book

University of Nebraska Press

1960

Library of Congress Catalog Card Number 60-12942.

Manufactured in the United States of America

Reprinted by arrangement with the Caxton Printers, Ltd.

First BISON BOOK edition published 1960

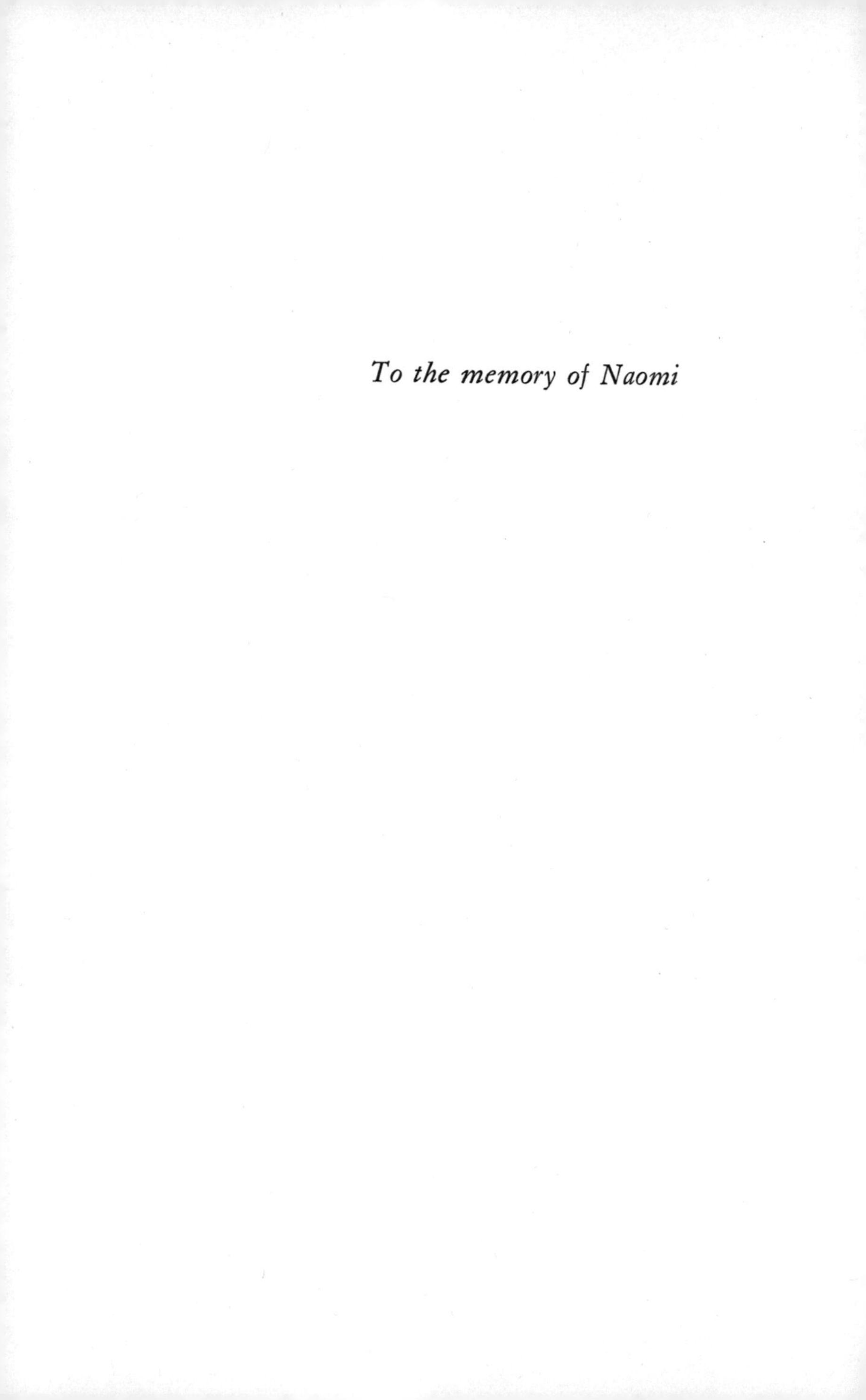

To the memory of Naomi

Introduction

The history of western railroad construction usually is written in terms of the building of the transcontinentals, with emphasis on the spectacular achievement by which the continent was first spanned by rail. After the dramatic ceremony of May 10, 1869, when the golden spike is driven on Promontory Summit, Utah, and the engines of the Union Pacific and the Central Pacific are brought together in a shower of champagne, the story of construction dwindles into a perfunctory account of the building of the other transcontinental lines. The major emphasis is reserved for the financial manueverings of the Goulds, the Hills, and the Harrimans, the rumblings of discontent emanating from the throats of the grangers, and the none-too-successful efforts of government to achieve some measure of control over the burgeoning railroad enterprise. Almost lost from sight is the fact that during the last three decades of the nineteenth century the story of construction is a major aspect of railroad history. This is particularly true of the Seventies and Eighties—the years between 1878 and 1888 saw more miles of track laid in the United States than any other similiar period in the country's history. Most of this construction was in the West, and much of it consisted of branch lines to support an ever-expanding population.

The publication in 1937 of James H. Kyner's memoirs provided a document which sheds light on this neglected phase of railroad history. Kyner was a railroad contractor who in the 1880's and 1890's built segments of various lines in Nebraska, Idaho, Colorado, and Wyoming. Just a recital of his contracts serves to illustrate the nature of the golden age of railroad expansion in the West.

His first contract, landed in 1881, was to construct twenty-five miles of a branch line of the Union Pacific being built up the Loup Valley from St. Paul, Nebraska, to serve settlers drawn to the area, in part at least, by railroad advertising. Next came work in Idaho on the Oregon Short Line, a subsidiary of the Union Pacific running from Granger, Wyoming, on the mail line, to Huntington, Oregon, where it connected with the Oregon Railroad and Navigation Company's line to Portland. The Oregon Short Line was built to develop the Pacific Northwest and to secure the region's trade for the Union Pacific. Subsequent contracts included work on the Denver, South Park and Pacific, which was to be absorbed into the system Jay Gould built to compete with the Union Pacific; the Fremont, Elkhorn and Missouri Valley, which funneled the trade of northwestern Nebraska, eastern Wyoming, and the Black Hills into Omaha (and which was bought by the Chicago and Northwestern almost as soon as it was built); the Colorado Midland, running across the mountains from Colorado Springs to Grand Junction; and the Denver and Rio Grande, pioneer of the narrow-gauge roads. Kyner also graded land for the Omaha Stockyards, did some work on a branch line of the Chicago, Burlington and Quincy near Creston, Iowa, and got involved in a disastrous railroad enterprise in Ohio known as the Lancaster and Hamden. His last major job was the development of a cut in Wyoming to make possible the relocation of part of the main line of the Union Pacific.

In writing his memoirs Kyner was preoccupied with the problems of construction, and the detail explaining how he solved these problems contributes greatly to the book's value as a primary source for the history of

American railroads. Kyner's concern with construction problems, it may be added, is perfectly understandable. When he took his first job, he was so inexperienced that he did not even know what was meant by the numbers on the surveyor's stakes. The cryptic "C.1.5" on the stake just beyond the railhead at the little village of St. Paul symbolized his dilemma. He writes:

> I stood there for a minute or more trying to interpret those hieroglyphics, but I could not. Had they been Latin or Greek I might have been able to recall enough of what I had been taught at college to make them out, but as it was I was utterly at sea. I had other things to bother me, however, and for the time being put that problem aside, coming back to it now and then and wondering how I could get its message interpreted without giving my own inexperience and ignorance away.

This little problem was by no means the only one faced by the neophyte contractor. He was as wanting in capital as he was in experience, and all of his supplies were obtained on credit. Somehow he solved his problems—big and little—and despite the unpropitious circumstances under which he began, he finished the job on time and cleared a profit of more than $10,000.

Self-made success of this type is not unique to the United States of the late nineteenth century, but it is difficult to imagine a time and place where it could have flourished more luxuriantly. Indeed, Kyner's career exhibited so much of the pragmatic enterprise which characterized the late nineteenth century in

America that his memoirs provide a valuable source for the study of that aspect of American life: having achieved success with neither training nor capital, he lost everything midway in his career and began all over again as a workman to rebuild his fortune.

Kyner dabbled in politics and served two terms in the Nebraska state legislature, where he was frankly a representative of the business interests of the state, particularly of the railroads. He first ran for the legislature at the suggestion of railroad leaders in Omaha who had been impressed with a speech he had made in David City in favor of a local railroad enterprise. The state constitution of 1875 had authorized the legislature to regulate railroads, but it was impossible to get effective regulatory measures passed. Representative Kyner was one of the reasons. He records: "Legislation adverse to the railroads was forever being proposed. During my four years in the legislature I opposed all this, with more than a little success. Not one adverse act was passed while I was there." His first railroad-building contract was a direct result of his course in the legislature—and he says so with disarming forthrightness. As a matter of fact, his candid discussion of the uncertain ground he walked between private interests and public responsibility is one of the principal values of Kyner's book and revelatory of aspects of the American mind during the expansive years of the late nineteenth century.

When Kyner first embarked on his memoirs he wrote with some diffidence: "If what I have to say is worth recording, it is because my youth and early manhood were spent while the strong and simple foundations of the present world were still unfinished. . . . The part that I have played has not been overwhelming. If what I have to say is worth the saying, it is merely because my memory is long."

His memory was long, and with the assistance of Hawthorne Daniel he translated it into a document which not only sheds light on business and politics but also contributes in a larger way to an understanding of the forces which built America, and particularly the American West. He tells of his boyhood in Ohio; of his service in the Civil War during which he lost a leg in the Battle of Shiloh; of his desultory efforts at higher education when invalided out; of his decision to go west; and of his early years in pioneer Nebraska. You cannot read Kyner's matter-of-fact account without gaining a clearer realization of what it was like to be young in America during the middle years of the nineteenth century.

When it appeared in 1937, *End of Track* received the Gold Medal Award of the Oregon Trail Association and it was widely and favorably reviewed. Writing in the *Mississippi Valley Historical Review,* Robert E. Riegel of Dartmouth College, an authority on the history of the West, said: "The book deserves a much wider public than that of specialists on the trans-Misisssippi railroads." It is hoped that this reprinting by the University of Nebraska Press will help to bring the book to that "much wider public" which it so eminently deserves.

JAMES C. OLSON

Author's Introduction

It is commonplace to say that men and women of great age recall the incidents of youth more clearly than the happenings of yesterday. Yet, unlike many commonplace remarks, this one is true. Nor need one feel that such a fact is hard to understand. The zest a person has in life grows somewhat less if he is nearly ninety, and the incidents of yesterday are merely unimportant repetitions of events from which, long since, the juice has been extracted. The days tick by like seconds of a clock, the very sound of which no longer seems to reach the ear.

Then, too, we older ones have lived throughout a

period of change, and the world in which we linger is not the one to which we came. We learned to live in other times than these—in simpler times to which we are attuned. We never were exotic plants, I know, and yet we do not like so much transplanting.

If what I have to say is worth recording, it is because my youth and early manhood were spent while the strong and simple foundations of the present world were still unfinished. I have no quarrel with a world that sometimes seems to me too complicated. Perhaps, however, in what I have to say, there may be an incident or two that will explain a little of those earlier times that have so powerfully impressed themselves upon our basic structure. Perhaps my "short and simple annals" may serve to record a portion of that sturdy past without which no such land as ours could ever have developed.

The part that I have played has not been overwhelming. If what I have to say is worth the saying, it is merely because by memory is long.

J. H.K.

1

NOTHING of which I know is dated from my birth except myself. Nor, as a matter of fact, is Lancaster, Ohio, during the years that immediately followed September 28, 1846, registered with unimpeachable accuracy in my mind. Youthful experiences, as I recall them, ordinarily seem to be adventures, and my adventures must have been few until 1853 when Father purchased the tavern in the little village of Oakland, twelve miles from Lancaster on the old Zanesville-Maysville Pike.

This pike was, in the 1850's, the one means of communication between Zanesville, Ohio, and Maysville, Kentucky. Along its forty-odd miles of length the stagecoach periodically rattled, stopping here and there at the villages and taverns past which the old road ran. Herds of cattle, of horses, and of hogs now and then crowded its narrow right of way as plodding farmers drove them on the long way to market at Cincinnati or at Baltimore. We school children, our bare feet begrimed with the deep dust of the road in spring and fall, or our cowhide boots crunching softly in the snow in winter, shouted and played as we made our unwilling way to the school at which Joe Harper taught, or whooped gleefully when we were released. We yelled as we scurried at every opportunity to the swimming hole, or walked more seriously, and much more slowly, home to perform the many chores that were our daily task.

The homes of the vicinity were simple, wholesome places, where pride of birth and position were unknown, where log houses, here and there, still told of earlier days, and where every soul for miles about, save one lone German immigrant, was of solid American colonial stock, to whom the Revolution and the War of 1812 were American history, of course, but were family history first.

The village of Oakland was never large, and yet was a town of consequence. It sprawled along both sides of the dusty pike, with one crossroad which had, I suppose, been the principal cause of the village's location, and among the two hundred-odd men, women, and children who made up the community there was not one whom I did not know.

The village tavern was, of course, the forum of the countryside—as truly as was the Roman Forum itself—and even as a child for whom the events of the vicinity were unimportant save as they affected me personally, I had an almost daily opportunity to hear the arguments between the local residents and farmers, who smoked their pipes and drank their beer and argued their points within the tavern or upon its wide two-storied porches.

The tavern itself stood at the crossroad, as was proper enough, for it was the very hub of the community, and at the corner, within arm's reach, stood the sign. A heavy post, buried firmly in the hard-packed earth, supported the metal bracket from which the sign hung, and the sign itself, bearing the single word "INN," bore also, on each side, the gilded likeness of a swan. Why no one ever thought to grease those metal supports I do not know, but they did not, and every breeze that blew set the gilded swan to rocking back and forth to the two-toned screech of rusty iron.

Along the pike the high two-storied porch ran the front length of the structure, the lower porch serving also as the sidewalk, and here, with horses drowsing sometimes in the hot sunlight, the arguments were endless. From this porch two doorways opened—one into the large old office, and one into the hall, from which, in turn, the parlor opened.

There were taverns in that day that left, I know, more than a little to be desired, but the inn at the sign of the Gilded Swan did not. For miles around—in Zanesville, in Lancaster, in Maysville—it was known for its hospitality, its food, its cleanliness. The porches in good weather, and the office in bad, were never empty. A drunken man about the place was almost unknown, and though a tiny room behind the office was called "the bar," it had no faint resemblance to any bar of later days. It contained, instead, merely a small supply of beer and whiskey, with now and then a bottle or two of wine upon its shelves. From this small supply a discreet amount was served in the office or upon the porch to those who called for it. Occasionally some visitor, who already had had his fair share of fiery waters elsewhere, called for more at the Gilded Swan, and I have often heard Father refuse it to them.

"I don't keep liquor here," he always told them, "for men to get drunk on."

And often, having thus refused one, he permitted some other person to be served, nor do I recall a single serious argument because of his rulings.

It is difficult, in days such as the ones in which we now live, to appreciate the possibility of such an inn living almost completely within itself. Coffee, salt, and a small number of other supplies, were, necessarily, purchased. Aside from these everything was produced locally, and large portions of the supplies were actually grown and prepared within the confines of the five acres that made up the inn grounds. All the vegetables were grown in the carefully tended garden. Pigs and chickens were as necessary a part of the economy of the place as beds and chairs. The old smokehouse was a treasure-trove of hams and sausages, and many a time, with my mind on other matters more important to a boy, have I too carelessly attended to my smokehouse duties and produced a temperature too high to suit the particular demands of my mother, whose many activities included the overseeing of almost everything having to do with the care and preparation of food.

Just how so busy a person as she ever managed to attend to all the duties to which she assigned herself I do not know. With six children one might think that her hands would have been full. Yet she attended to such duties in addition as few women these days have even the faintest knowledge of. The wood ashes were saved for their part in the making of soap. The big spinning wheel seemed always to require her busy hand. The garden constantly demanded her efficient oversight. The linen in such a place must continually be replenished, mended, washed, and ironed. The meals that were customary in those days were of such tremendous proportions as to defy description, with apple butter and jelly, pickles and preserves, in never-ending profusion. It is true that in the huge dining room, to which one went through a tremendously wide quadruple door leading from the parlor, the meals were simply served or, perhaps more accurately, were not served at all. The tables were set, the food was brought on in great steaming dishes, the dinner bell was rung, and thereafter, for the most part, the guests were left to their own devices, save for the refilling of coffee cups, the renewal of empty serving dishes, and the hospitable urging of the hostess.

The great loaves of bread, fresh from the oven, faded away with astonishing speed. The mountains of potatoes, the vast supplies of butter and marmalade, the bushels of peas and beans fresh from the garden went to supply such appetites as rarely exist in these much later days.

The table manners that were proper enough within the dining room of the Gilded Swan would, I know, hardly pass muster in the Waldorf-Astorias of today, but what would seem unduly crude now was proper enough in 1855. How, for instance, could peas be eaten with a two-tined fork? They couldn't, and the knife was the implement that was properly utilized. How could scalding coffee be urged down human throats? Why, only by pouring it out into the deep and commodious saucers, where it could more readily cool—saucers made, by the way, with that in mind.

Table silver was not then in common use, and the knives and forks were finely made of steel. The spoons were pewter, as the sugar bowl, the spoon holder, and other pieces of tableware were. The china wasn't china at all, but porcelain, or if it were china—and the Gilded Swan had more than a little fine old willowware and other pieces generations old—it was kept out of the hands of hungry guests, and set on shelves in crowded cupboards to keep it safe from harm.

The dining room of the Gilded Swan was a handsome place for Ohio in that day, with a gayly colored rag carpet of mammoth proportions covering every square inch of its floor. It was not common in such taverns to use white tablecloths and napkins, yet Mother's table linen was always white—and spotless until the meal was well along.

And when the surfeited guests pushed back their chairs and rose, they could rest at their ease in a parlor where mahogany furniture rubbed elbows with simpler stuff; where an ingrain carpet—rich enough, we thought, for kings—and prettily papered walls set off the white handmade doors and woodwork very daintily, indeed; where a magnificent rosewood grandfather's clock ponderously ticked the time. That huge old clock was, I believe, the handsomest I have ever seen, and one of the largest as well. A hundred times, when we played at hide-and-seek, I have crouched silently within its commodious base, with the pendulum and the big weights above my head. Had the old inn and its furnishings remained intact until today, what an antique dealer's heaven it would have been, but the furnishings, the heavy locks and great H hinges, some of which were made by Father himself, attracted little enough attention then. I have often wished of late, however, that I might have kept a pair of those old hinges.

Nor, in these days of flower gardens, need one think that flowers weren't appreciated then. In the great brick-paved court, on three sides of which the Gilded Swan was built, was such a garden as I have seldom seen. A rosebush—not a climber or a rambler—stood as high as the roof of the upstairs porch, which ran about on two sides of the old court, and all across one side of the court a bed of old-fashioned flowers bloomed brightly under the care of Mother's ever-busy hands. The well, too, stood beneath a roof extended from the woodshed, and the overflow served to supply a horse trough in the street that ran beside the inn. The horse troughs of that day, of course, were almost as numerous as the filling stations of a later age, but, thank Heaven, they were rarely painted red.

The Gilded Swan was of some importance in those days, in part because the stagecoach used it as a terminus. Each morning, harnessing his horses to the stage, John Erie mounted to his seat, and placing the mail pouches underneath his feet, called for whatever passengers were bound for Circleville and the railroad. As early dusk approached, the stage returned to spend the night at the Gilded Swan, and, more important, to bring the news of what was happening in the world. Then it was that the men of the town were wont to congregate in greatest numbers to talk of politics, of slavery, of legislation in Columbus or in Washington—to argue, always to argue, the many urgent problems of the day.

The whole of all that country for miles about had long ago been settled by veterans of the Revolution and the War of 1812. Revolutionary figures had, of course, by my time, largely faded from the picture, but many were the sons and daughters of those who had fought at Brandywine, at Saratoga, and at Yorktown. Our own family had been well represented in the Revolution, at least four great-uncles and grandfathers having worn the Continental uniform. But though the Revolutionary generation was no longer with us, the veterans of Hull's surrender at Detroit were numerous in Oakland. I was forever hearing of that march across the thousand flooded streams to reach Detroit, only to be ended by surrender without an effort at offense. Each year, on August 16, that surrender was recalled. All through the day the veterans of that ill-starred march would come by ones and twos to the porches and the office of the Gilded Swan. All day they told of wading streams, of sleeping on the soggy, rain-soaked ground, of going hungry and of struggling through, and of being surrendered without a bullet singing by. How bitter they always were, and what blackguard names they flung at Hull and his surrender!

The Mexican War was then, of course, a thing of merely yesterday, and more than a few of those in Oakland had been at the storming of Chapultapec and elsewhere. What boy could fail to drink in all the yarns they spun? And when the wars with other nations were not being discussed again, the Indian troubles of an earlier day were perfect sources for a thousand fascinating tales, while from the farther West, came yarns of hunters, trappers, fighters of a dozen kinds.

The folk who traveled through so small a place as Oakland were, of course, not numerous. Peddlers came from time to time, and tinware peddlers, with their fascinating wagons heaped with shiny ware, were especially welcome. They sold their stuff for money, of course, but they traded it, as well, for old brass and copper, and for rags. Now and then a wagon filled with notions came—thread, needles, odds and ends. Hucksters, out to purchase eggs and butter, came sometimes; drovers with herds of cattle, on the way to Baltimore, were common guests at the Gilded Swan. Now and then a traveling salesman came to induce, if possible, George Hamlin and Bernard Kiefaver, the keepers of the general stores in Oakland, to purchase more supplies to add to the assortments already on their shelves.

Such visitors, of course, were fascinating to such a boy as I, but it was not always possible to see them. The school to which we went was half a mile beyond the creek where we went swimming, and there we sat for hours and hours, sometimes when more exciting things were happening about the office or the stables of the Gilded Swan.

The school was new in my day—a white frame structure with an entry and a single room. The class included youngsters of every age, of course, from little tykes of five or six to great big gawky boys and girls too large for the benches. I suspect that pedagogy has improved somewhat since those days when Joe Harper, whom Father, as a member of the school board, had found in Amanda, ruled us with a never-ending supply of sharp birch switches ever ready at his hand. And yet, of all the instructors I ever had, I most clearly remember Harper. The simple things he taught us we remembered, and if his own education was not so broad as it should have been, he taught us well. In later days more learned professors taught me infinitely less, I know.

How often I have seen him, when we were supposed to be conning the lessons he had assigned, take his penknife from his pocket and, choosing from a great collection of goose quills in a container before him, carefully cut the pens with which he taught us to write. And how often, when my heavy hand had sprung the quill too far, would he repair it for me.

Our school was far from crude, one room though it was. The teacher sat behind his desk upon a platform. To one side sat a square box stove, into which in winter went great quantities of wood. Beneath it, oftentimes, our wet woolen mittens lay to dry, while we, at wooden desks not greatly different from those in use today, carved our initials as we hid behind our books, or played the pranks that boys have always played since schools began.

Half the room was occupied by boys, the other half by girls. Such segregation seemed to us entirely natural and proper, though what ideas had inspired it I cannot now imagine. There even were two doors—one for each sex—by which we entered from the smaller entryway, though for communicating with the world outdoors one door served well enough for all of us.

It was down a hill not far from school that we coasted on our homemade sleds. The swimming hole of warmer days was near at hand as well, while Dustman's stone quarry, hardly fifty yards from the swimming hole, was a place no boy in the vicinity could resist. Long since it had been abandoned, but still there were abrupt rock faces we could climb, flat stone shelves upon which we could bask in the spring sunshine, and innumerable places here and there such as make their resistless claim upon the imagination of every boy.

The 1850's were, of course, a period of flux. Slavery was a never-ending source of discussion. No later problem of which I know ever went so deeply into the hearts of everyone. Discussion of the subject was forever rife, and though abolitionists were rare in Oakland, the broad porches of the Gilded Swan often heard both sides of the problem discussed.

My father was a quiet man, not given to many words. I never saw him excited, and years later a major of the regiment with which Father served at Gettysburg and throughout Sherman's March to the Sea, told me that no other man he knew was so competent in times of danger as John Kyner. In the perennial and sometimes angry discussions in and about the Gilded Swan, Father took but little part. On one occasion I saw him quietly knock Jake Hedges down, when Jake, having come in from

Tarleton half-seas over, grew foul in his abuse. But even that, which frightened me so at the time, was done quietly and without heat, and once the bawling fellow had been felled, Father as quietly lifted him to his feet, and pushed him through the door, where someone else saw to it that he left.

Father took his politics as quietly as he took everything else, but like almost everyone else in the community, he was a Democrat, in favor of slavery. I doubt if he would have dreamed of owning a slave himself, even if the laws of Ohio had permitted it, but he believed quite firmly that the Negroes were not fitted to take their places as citizens, that slavery was an institution which, while it made possible certain injustices, nevertheless served the Negro better than freedom could. It was, I believe, the opinion most commonly held in our community. Certainly outright abolition was almost unsupported, George Hamlin, the owner of Oakland's principal general store, being the only exception in the little town.

Three years is almost an eternity in the life of a child, and by the time we had lived in Oakland that long, I was part and parcel of the place. Every landmark in the vicinity was familiar to me. The name of every person was ready on my tongue. I had played countless times amid the fragrant shavings of Jim Shafer's cooper shop, and watched him and his employees put their barrels and kegs and tubs together. I had been into the woods to watch the shingle makers work, to look on while rail splitters drove their wedges into the tough logs. I knew the blacksmith shops, and loved to watch the great bare-armed men as they pumped their vast bellows and shaped their horseshoes. I had leaped into the hay from the top of every hayloft, and searched for huckleberries in every likely place from the village to Dustman's deserted quarry and beyond. But though I knew all Oakland as only a boy can know a place, I had never at all appreciated the depth of feeling that lay behind the arguments that were forever being renewed upon the porches and in the office of the tavern. The words were quite familiar by now, but slavery—that ever-present subject—had never touched me. The "South," to me, was as distant land, with problems, customs, beliefs too strange and far away to come close home to me.

But then, in the spring of 1856, when I had reached the age of nine, an incident occurred that suddenly created in my childish mind an impression so vivid that somehow I instantly grew in mental stature, and reached a conclusion all my own—for the first time, perhaps, in my nine years of life.

I had been to school, and coming home as usual, saw, far along the road ahead of me, a crowd of people gathered at the tavern. Horses were tied to the hitching rail, and groups of men were gathered here and there. My first thought was that there had been a fox hunt. Thinking about some of the yarns the hunters would tell, I broke into a run in order not to miss them.

As I came closer, however, I saw there were no hounds, and noted, too, that among this gathering of people there were no laughs or smiles. Everyone was talking, and obviously there was much excitement, but though I crowded in among the groups no one answered my insistent questions. I saw two men I did not know—men who did not live in Oakland. Working farther through the crowd, I finally found a young Negro sitting near the office door. His pants, I noticed, were torn off at the knees. His feet were bare. His shirt, which had no sleeves, was open at the throat. But it was not his ragged costume that intrigued me. I had seen others in clothes not greatly better. What *did* attract my interest were the iron rings about his ankles and the chain that ran between them.

Was this a criminal? I wondered. Had he stolen something? Killed someone? I tried to get a man near by to tell me, but he was busy talking. I looked about and saw my mother, and though she too was excited, I finally got her attention.

"What's he done?" I asked. "What's he done? Something wrong? Has he hurt somebody?"

She shook her head.

"No, Jim," she replied. "He's hurt no one. He's a slave, and he's run away from his master."

"And they came after him?" I asked.

She nodded.

"Where did they catch him?" I demanded.

"Down in Dustman's quarry," she replied, her attention on a conversation going on near by.

"What will they do with him?" I went on.

"They are going to take him back to his master in Kentucky," she replied absently.

"Well, what are the people making such a fuss about?" I asked, and finally she turned to me. She told me that some of the people did not want to let him be taken back, that some among them were insisting that he be released.

I had heard of slavery and slaves, of course, but this was the first slave I had ever seen. It was only natural that I should go nearer to the ragged, shackled Negro, at whom I stared and stared, my mind vaguely troubled and unclear. It occurred to me then that someone owned this Negro, just as Father owned old Joe, our favorite horse.

That vaguely troubled me. As I stood there thinking of his being owned as if he were an animal, I noticed that he had tears in his eyes, that now and then one welled out and ran down across his black cheek. He was, as I have said, a young Negro—hardly more than a boy himself—and drawing closer still I spoke to him.

"Boy," I asked, "what you crying for?"

He did not answer. Boylike, I asked again. But not until I had asked a third time did he look up. Even then he looked at one of the strangers, who was standing near, before he answered me. Perhaps he would not have answered then, save that the fellow's back was turned.

I asked again, and he turned toward me, a tear still glistening upon his black cheek.

"Ah wants to be free," he replied softly. "Ah wants to be free, like you is."

A lump seemed to come into my throat. I now heard some of our neighbors as they objected to his being taken. I remember Mr. Bowers, who owned one of the cooper shops, saying over and over, "They *shan't* take him away. They *shan't* take him away."

But now the constable came, and with him came Squire Lindsay. It was the squire who said that the Ohio Fugitive Slave Law not only gave the owners of runaway slaves the right to recapture them, but required the citizens of Ohio to assist if necessary or be guilty of contempt of court.

The men from Kentucky mounted their horses presently. With the shackled Negro walking between them, they set off along the pike toward Maysville, while I, troubled and ill at ease, stared after them.

My father, I knew, had always held that slavery was justified. Everyone in the community, excepting only

George Hamlin, felt much as he did. Yet here among the crowd that had gathered there were many who had opposed that Negro's return to his Kentucky master.

Why? I asked myself. Why? Why, if slavery was right, should he *not* go? And suddenly I knew. It was *not* right. Their arguments were faulty. The thing was wrong.

I walked out into the dusty pike and stared after those two disappearing horsemen and at the shackled figure that still walked there between them. In that very moment, there on the Zanesville-Maysville Pike, I, at the age of nine, became an abolitionist.

2

THERE may have been parts of the country where the abolitionists were numerous enough to miss the unpopularity they had around Oakland, but I know nothing of that. I merely know that George Hamlin was the only adult abolitionist in the village and that he was supported by no one save his own two sons and myself. Inasmuch as Charlie Hamlin was about my age, while Hannibal, whom we called Yank, was younger, Mr. Hamlin's supporters can hardly be said to have carried much weight. A part of what we lacked, however, in importance we made up in enthusiasm, and soon had become a little group of social outcasts, who gloried in the anathemas hurled at us by our Whig and Democratic playmates, exchanging black eyes and bloody noses the while. The other boys at school outnumbered us so greatly that at times our lives were miserable, and even the girls, turning on us, pointed their fingers and shouted: "Nigger, nigger, nigger."

Both the Hamlin boys underwent all this as well as I, but they, at least, found sympathy at home. Not so I. Father, it is true, was quiet enough, as always, and my brothers and sisters, being younger than I, had little to say, but Mother boxed my ears more than once when, unbidden, I entered some discussion at the inn with my own weak arguments or paraphrases of those I had heard Mr. Hamlin advance.

It was in the autumn of 1856 that the presidential campaign was fought, and the excitement of those days was endless. The Democrats had nominated Buchanan and Breckinridge, and as the campaign grew in intensity, a tall hickory pole was set up beside the sign of the Gilded Swan, in order that an American flag and a great streamer bearing the names of the Democratic candidates could be flung to the Oakland breezes.

The Whigs, of course, were a party of the past, and out of their remnants, together with a scattering of Free-Soilers, independent Democrats and others, a new party had been organized. Fremont and Dayton were their candidates, and while they were not called abolitionists, the abolitionists supported them. As I recall it, the party of Fremont and Dayton was most commonly spoken of as the Independent. Certainly it was not until much later that the people about Oakland called it Republican.

In a community as strongly Democratic as Oakland was, the Independents were a small minority indeed. Still, they far outnumbered Mr. Hamlin and his three youthful abolitionist associates, with the result that our youthful political battles, while still one-sided, were not such as to leave the three of us alone. I verily believe that some of the boys with Free-Soil fathers looked askance at the three of us who so boldly declared for abolition. But though they gave us less than absolute support in our beliefs, they were native sons of Ohio, which seemed to make them politically practical, with the result that they were willing to accept the support even of us three whom, otherwise, they barely countenanced at all.

The campaign in the country around was growing

more and more furious, and in Oakland no one had dared to put up a pole carrying a streamer marked for Fremont and Dayton, when a big wagon loaded with men, drawn by six horses, and followed by a long string of other vehicles, drove past the inn on the way to a rally that was to be held in Lancaster. A crowd was standing on the tavern porch as the vehicles went by, my mother and I among the rest.

Beside the inn the tall pole stood, flaunting the Buchanan streamer out above the street, and as the six-horse wagon with its load of men approached, the men within it waved their hats in approval of the streamer, shouting their hurrahs for Buchanan and Breckinridge. As I recall it not a voice was raised for Fremont. Certainly I heard none. I felt it necessary, consequently, to voice my sentiments, and in my loudest voice, which, high and thin, had certain powers of penetration, I shouted.

"Hurrah!" I cried, "for Fremont and Dayton!"

So surprising a shout in that gathering of fervent Democrats was enough to attract more than one eye to the youthful perpetrator, but I had not a moment in which to enjoy the spotlight when Mother's hand, which could be heavy on occasion, descended with a resounding whack upon my ear.

"Hit him again!" bawled someone from the wagon. "Hit him again!"

But I had scurried beyond the reach of Mother's hand, angry with treatment so unfair, and anxious to talk over a suddenly matured plan of mine for furthering Fremont's election.

My plan was merely to erect another pole, and to fly from it a streamer bearing the names of Fremont and Dayton. To erect the pole was, of course, a task that could, in a pinch, be managed by the two Hamlin boys and myself. The streamer was another matter. However, presenting the problem to Mrs. Hamlin, it was solved at once by her announcement that she would donate the streamer. She started it at once, while we, armed with an axe, went off to find our pole. We found it finally—a pole of sassafras—well out in the woods. We cut it down, which was not difficult, and having lopped off the branches we dragged that heavy pole a good half mile to town. There beside the pike, about midway between the Hamlin home and the Hamlin store, we nailed our colors to it, and set the tall pole up.

We were, I can assure you, a proud and happy trio, but early the next morning Charlie came to the Gilded Swan, and finding me, told me that the pole was down. I went with him at once, of course, and there it was upon the ground, with the flag torn up and smeared with mud. Our instant decision was to erect it once more, but Mr. Hamlin, showing us some damage that had been done to the front door of his store, advised us to let the matter rest.

Buchanan was elected, of course, and for a time matters went more smoothly in Oakland, though the problem of slavery was ever growing more difficult to solve, and constantly from Washington came reports that grew more serious as the months passed by.

The next four years passed slowly. We made sugar in the early spring. We planted our gardens and smoked our meat. We spun and repaired and performed those many endless tasks that such an establishment as the Gilded Swan required. The village changed but little, though that little was adverse to the welfare of the inn.

Amanda, three miles away to the northeast; Stoutsville, two and a half miles west; Tarleton, three miles south—all were attracting the farmers of the region away from Oakland. The Gilded Swan still maintained its reputation, and for miles about the groups who arranged for parties and for dances still came often to our tavern. But such a hostelry could not be prosperous on parties and on dances. The steady streams of visitors on whom the inn had counted were growing smaller, at first so slowly that we hardly noticed it.

During all this period, the Gilded Swan was periodically the scene of an irregular series of social events that had long since come to be called "rat-tail suppers." When and where these events had originated or how wide their vogue was I do not know, but among the people of our portion of Ohio they were highly popular. At Oakland, as well as at all the near-by villages, they were an important part of the life of the people.

The name does not mean that rat tails were on the menu. As a matter of fact not a single rat tail was to be seen at these gatherings. They played an important part, however, in the proceedings that culminated in the suppers, as I shall explain.

Ohio was, of course, almost entirely rural at the time of which I am telling, and the Federal and state departments of agriculture had not grown into such ponderous and inexcusably extravagant agencies as they have now come to be. The result was that the farmers had to face their own difficulties and overcome them as best they could without the assistance of corps of tax-consuming men from Columbus or from Washington.

Now one of the pests that had come to be exceedingly troublesome was the rat. It did all sorts of damage, and no amount of effort on the part of an individual farmer served to rid his farm of the pest. It was obviously a problem for unified action, and the people of the region, being nothing if not practical, developed an idea that made rat catching a sport and a contest instead of a difficult and a thankless task.

The idea was as follows:

A meeting would be called at which two men were chosen as the heads of the two contesting sides. These two men drew up a list of all the men of the district who could be counted upon to take part, and from the list they chose alternately, until two sides, equal in numbers, had been made up. The total number might be of any size, but usually the ones of which I knew numbered from thirty to forty.

With the sides chosen, a date for a supper was selected, to be held in two or three or even four weeks. In the time that intervened, each of the two contending sides did their utmost to kill rats, the tail from each slain rat constituting the evidence of his demise. On the afternoon of the day the supper was to be held, representatives of the contending sides, each with their collections of rat tails, would assemble at the stable of the Gilded Swan, where the trophies would be counted, the side with the smaller number of rat tails being saddled with the cost of the supper.

Every man engaged was permitted to bring his wife or his sweetheart to the supper, which made a gathering of considerable dimensions. Furthermore, these suppers were not attended by dyspeptics. For days the kitchen of the Gilded Swan would have been preparing. Cakes and pies of a dozen kinds were baked with the most amazing care. Meat, poultry, potatoes, peas, beans, cabbage, tomatoes, corn, and every other edible that was in season were on the menu. Bread, biscuits, rolls, honey, marmalade, jelly, jam, pickles, preserves—all were crowded upon the gleaming tablecloths. The largest serving dishes were brought out, to be refilled many times from the great supplies in the kitchen. The dining room was lighted by scores of extra candles and all the lard lamps that could be spared from other rooms. Uproarious good humor filled the big old room with sound, and once the food had been consumed and the guests had withdrawn to parlor, office, porch, and court, the dining room was cleared of dishes and of furniture, and the orchestra was given a place near the fireplace.

A fiddle or two, a cornet, perhaps a guitar, and certainly a bass viol were set to work, and from then until the wee sma' hours merriment reigned. Waltzes, Virginia reels, cotillions, followed one after another in rapid succession until, finally, with their wives or sweethearts beside them in buggies or in wagons, or behind them on horseback, victors and vanquished in the jolly war on rats scattered to their farms and homes.

Such affairs were profitable, of course, to the Gilded Swan, but they were periodical at best. They lasted on into the terrible years of the Civil War, but they did not serve to replace the gradual diminution of trade that was due to the competition of the near-by towns through which the railroad passed, leaving Oakland in a gradually fading backwater of trade.

Still the inn served as the clearinghouse for news, and still upon its porches the endless arguments continued. The campaign of 1860 was bitter and exciting, and the election of Lincoln was far less popular than it might well have been in Oakland. But now the news that came to

Oakland each time the stage arrived grew vastly more exciting: the brawls and fights in Congress; the hot-headed demands and speeches of certain Southerners; the Ordinance of Secession passed by South Carolina; the occupation of Fort Sumter by Major Anderson. Faster and faster moved these serious events. More and more excitement was engendered. The *Star of the West,* sent to supply Fort Sumter, was fired upon in Charleston Harbor and forced to turn back. That was in January, and well do I recall the day the news arrived.

It had been cold—sharply cold—since the night before, with a hard cold sky, like steel, above our heads. In the afternoon the clouds obscured the sun, and as evening came, a powdering of snow had covered the pike, while the cold wind blew the flakes in windrows along the cold and open porch. The fireplaces in the office and the parlor were blazing brightly. The candles and the old lard lamps were lighted early, and half an hour or so before the stage was due, the office was well filled with those who had come to wait until John Erie should arrive with whatever news there might be.

I was engaged in adding a great piece of wood, almost too heavy for me, to the office fire, lifting it over the tall andirons, when, from down the frozen road, I heard the rattle of horses' feet, heard the well-known sound of the stagecoach wheels, heard John Erie's voice as the stage pulled up outside the door.

The log was awkward, and I had my task half done. I could not leave it, but that John had brought some news of more than ordinary interest, I knew. I struggled with the log, as all the waiting men in the office left their mugs of beer and hurried to the door. A cold breeze blew across the floor as they crowded out, and with it came John's voice again.

"They've fired upon a ship in Charleston Harbor," I heard him shout above the questions that were being showered upon him.

I gave the log a push, let it fall with a crash that set the sparks to flying up the chimney, and ran out with the rest. Everyone was talking. Everyone was asking questions. No one was listening. But presently John pushed his way inside, the crowd about him. Voices were loud, excited. Few had heard, as yet, just what he had to say, and someone, as interested as the rest, but less excited, raised his voice.

"Hold on," he cried. "Hold on. Let John tell what he knows. Don't everybody talk at once."

John pulled off his mittens and unwound the muffler that was around his neck and over his head. The driver's seat on the old stage was an exposed, cold place on such a night.

"They told me in Circleville," he began, "that a ship named the *Star of the West* that was goin' in to Charleston Harbor with some supplies for Major Anderson in Fort Sumter was fired on by the secessionists."

A flurry of voices drowned him out as new visitors, coming in a constant stream, crowded into the office until hardly standing room was left. The log I had put on the fire popped like a musket, and a burning coal, blown out, singed a dog that stood there among those booted feet. A yelp of pain broke from him, and someone drove him out.

"Go on, John," shouted a voice.

"The ship had to turn around and git out," added John. "That's all I know."

The flurry of talk that broke out now filled the room with sound. A few hurried out to carry the news elsewhere, but most of the people stayed, and more kept coming. I even saw McGee, our stableman, among the crowd instead of attending to his duties of putting Erie's team up. Louise Myers, our cook, came in, her apron flecked with flour, probably from biscuits she was making.

"Does it mean war?" asked some.

"They need a thrashing," insisted someone else.

"What'll Buchanan do?" asked a third.

"Nothin'," cried someone, evidently not a Democrat. "He'll do nothin', and let things go 'til Lincoln's in."

Supper in the dining room was delayed that night, I remember, a thing unusual enough at the Gilded Swan to impress itself upon my memory, and even when the bell was rung, the dining room filled slowly, while in the office and in the parlor the booted men stood talking seriously until very late.

All Oakland was wrought up during the weeks that followed: the entire nation was, I suppose. A group of soldiers appeared not long thereafter, driving a wagon and demanding all the muskets that the discharged soldiers of the Mexican War had brought home with them. There was one such musket at the Gilded Swan—though whose it had been I do not know—and when it was brought out and put into the wagon, I climbed upon a wheel and looked within. There lay the muskets, together with a great curved sword, the like of which I had never seen before. Later I was to learn that it was a cavalry sabre.

Every few days more news came about the tense situation at Charleston, where Major Anderson, with his pitiful handful of badly supplied men, was holding Fort

Sumter, while all about were forts and batteries that finally were seized by the secessionists. Then Lincoln was inaugurated, and a month or so later came the news that Sumter had been fired upon. And John Erie was not the man who brought the word this time.

Doctor Shafer was the one physician of Oakland. He had been called to the vicinity of Stoutsville, two or three miles away, after Erie had brought the stage in for the night. Having attended to his patient, he stopped at the Stoutsville telegraph office before coming home, in the hope of getting some news. And at the very moment he entered, the operator was receiving a message that told meagerly that Sumter had been fired upon, and that even at that moment was under fire.

I suppose that the distance from Stoutsville to Oakland had not often been covered in less time than Dr. Shafer took that night. He drove a two-wheeled sulky, with one of the town's best horses between the shafts. The gathering at the Gilded Swan had largely melted away by the time we heard the doctor's voice shouting in the distance, for John Erie's news had not been much that night. But now, suddenly, from down the road that crossed the pike we heard the doctor's voice, and heard, too, the pounding of his horse's hoofs, the rattle of the sulky as its steel tires struck the stones upon the way.

I was on my way upstairs to bed, I remember, and stopped midway on the stairs when I heard his booming voice. What he was saying I did not know, but I knew his voice and knew him. He was not one to go shouting along the roads at night unless he had something of importance to impart.

There was a rush through the hall below me, for some of those in the office hurried out that way. I heard voices and the sound of feet upon the porch, and scurried down the stairs to learn what was happening. The door from the hall to the porch was open, letting in the pleasant April breeze, and as I hurried out to where a dozen men were crowding on the porch, the doctor's sulky drew up before the porch and stopped.

"They've fired on Sumter!" he shouted in his great bass voice. "They've fired on Sumter, and Anderson is firing back."

If the news of the *Star of the West* had excited Oakland, it was nothing to what happened now. Like an anthill broken open, the village suddenly seethed with running people. Men and women hurried toward the tavern. Tousled children, obviously fresh from bed, came trooping out, their dresses and their roundabouts awkwardly fastened. The evening was not cold, and the porch of the inn was crowded within five minutes, the faint light from the candles and the lard lamps in the office and the parlor lighting the milling people vaguely through the open doors and the partly shaded windows.

War! War! War! was the talk of everyone. One loud-mouthed fellow, whose name I have forgotten, but who later served almost four years in the war to come, bawled out that he could take a bunch of school children and lick those secessionists with cornstalks. Later, I suppose he changed his mind on that point. For half the night the crowd milled about the Gilded Swan, and finally left us, still excited, to talk at home for hours to come.

And now, of course, the tidal wave of war swept over us: Lincoln's call for three-month volunteers; troops fired upon in Baltimore; the setting-up of the Confederate government; the burning of the Navy Yard at Norfolk; the Battle of Bull Run.

I was fourteen, and all this news of war so fascinated me that I could think of nothing else. What is it that makes every boy that age want so to grasp a gun? His sense of chivalry and desire for adventure, I suppose; yes, and the romance that always has been used to drape the sordidness and awfulness of war.

It was long before those three-month volunteers had served their terms that everyone could see that this war was only now beginning. By early autumn more calls for volunteers were out—three-year terms this time. It was quite a step from three months, and still not long enough, though no one guessed it at the time.

Father, two years before, had gone to California, leaving Mother alone to operate the Gilded Swan. It was not an easy task, especially now, for the towns about had taken so much away from Oakland, and the war, almost immediately, took the rest. And I, fifteen in September, and the oldest child, should have stayed at home to help. Yet the war was in my blood. Already most of the men of Oakland had gone. Furthermore, boys of fifteen are likely to be foolhardy, harebrained creatures. I was, I know.

I said enough about it, I am sure, but how could a mother as troubled and busy as mine take such talk seriously? Undoubtedly she did not dream that any recruiting sergeant would take a boy my age. Furthermore, I have no doubt that in her eyes I was far more youthful than I seemed to others.

It was on the tenth of October, 1861, that I climbed into a wagon belonging to a farmer who was on his way to Lancaster, and saying nothing to anyone in Oakland, went with him across the twelve long miles to the larger town. Just what was in my mind, I do not know with certainty. I only know that vaguely I had decided to enlist.

In Lancaster, where I had often been before, I had no trouble locating the man who was recruiting for the 46th Ohio Infantry, and when I found him I asked how old a fellow had to be to enlist. He replied that eighteen years was the minimum age, whereupon I told him I had had my eighteenth birthday the month before.

He knew better, I am certain, for later I found that he had put me down as seventeen, but he raised no difficulties. I wrote my name down on a blank, and after an hour or so of waiting was mustered in.

For three days I was kept waiting in Lancaster, and then, with another boy named Charlie Townsend, was bundled on the stage for Columbus in charge of a young man from the recruiting office who was to see that we reached our destination. The stage took us to Columbus, and from there we walked nine miles to camp, which was at Worthington, in Franklin County.

I was tired when finally we came in sight of camp, but what a thrill of delight ran through me when I saw rows and rows of bright, white tents, the flag upon the tall and slender pole, and the parade grounds, all bright and clean and fresh in the clear sunlight!

We were taken to our captain's tent, and an orderly assigned us to our quarters. There were already three men from Oakland in the company to which I was assigned, and I was told to share their tent. I knew them all, of course—Jack and Ad Neigh, the sons of a veteran of the Mexican War who had lost an arm at Buena Vista, and Jake Root, a boy not over twenty.

No boy of fifteen finds it difficult to fit into such a life. Within a day or two I felt as much at home as many of the older men who had been there longer. We rose to reveille, fell in for roll call, made our beds upon the straw we spread upon the ground, drilled in squads, in companies, and finally in battalions. Now and then we marched a few miles about the near-by roads. We had inspection, dress parade, and guard mount. All of this we did without a uniform save those the officers wore, while all of us used sticks for the muskets that had not come.

We waited weeks for uniforms, but finally they came. A buzz of excitement ran through the company streets as a long train of army wagons entered camp, piled high with boxes. Scores of men were busy for a day in the old mill that served as the quartermaster's store, and then, company by company, we were ordered out, to get the uniforms that meant so much to all of us.

We were marched in through the wide mill door between two rows of great boxes upon which lay the long-delayed equipment. Our captain shouted out his order (how plainly I remember it): "Front rank stand fast! Rear rank about face!" And there, having eased off a bit to right and left, each of us found himself before a pile of clothing. No one thought of sizes. Uniforms were there, and underwear and shirts. Shoes, socks, leathern stocks, and all the rest. If they didn't fit, that was our affair. Trade with someone. That was all.

When I got back to our tent I could not wait to don that uniform. And what an outfit it turned out to be! I verily believe that I recall every single item in it.

They were as follows:

A hat.

A cap.

Two flannel shirts.

Two undershirts.
Two pair of drawers.
Two pair of woolen socks.
One pair of shoes.
One pair of sky-blue pants.
One dark-blue blouse.
One dress coat (a garment for a monkey,
I am sure).
One leathern stock.

Several items in this wardrobe intrigued me mightily. Folk these days may not realize that underwear is of fairly recent introduction. In Oakland we boys knew nothing of it. Our pants and shirts and roundabouts were washable, and they were often washed you can be sure. In winter, lining to our pants served to keep us warm. What use for underwear then?

But here before me lay these garments which fitted like the paper on the wall. They were more like tights that I had seen in circuses than like anything else I knew. The result was that, having donned them, I went into the company street and turned a handspring or two in veritable joy, and probably in emulation of the acrobats whom I had seen.

But there was that leathern stock. I did not know at all what it could be, until someone told me it was like a necktie, but being stiff and strong as any dog collar, it served right well to make us hold our heads erect.

With that settled, I turned my attention to my uniform, and tried to get it on. With the galluses that had held my old pants up, I put those sky-blue trousers on. They were, I felt, somewhat too long, and so I buckled up my galluses until the waistband of those trousers was just beneath my arms. Still my feet were well within them, and not until I had turned the pants up some inches at the bottom could I get my feet into the heavy cowhide shoes.

Finally, however, I pulled on my dress coat, set the wide-brimmed, feather-decorated hard hat on my head, and, proud beyond words of every ridiculous and ill-fitting thing about that outfit, went out and paraded delightedly up and down our company street, the leathern stock all but choking me, the brass on my hat shining in the sun, the six brass buttons on the short tail of my dress blouse bobbing as I walked, and those much-turned-up sky-blue trousers flapping about my too large shoes.

The muskets came much later, after we had traded back and forth with trousers, shoes, and hats until we were reasonably well fitted. And with the guns came belts, shoulder straps, cap boxes, bayonets, all made of, or carried in, heavy black leather, decorated with brass plates marked with eagles and with stars.

The guns we got were Belgian muskets, and what weapons they were! Long, heavy, with steel ramrods and plenty of brass straps to hold them together. Mine was, of course, no heavier than any of the rest, but it was far too heavy for me to aim, save by bending far backward and resting my elbow on my hip. With the butt on the ground, the muzzle was just level with my eyes.

When, days later, we had learned a little of the manual of arms, we were taken out first to fire those guns. Mine hit me so hard upon the shoulder and jaw that it knocked me down. Nor was I the only one.

From the middle of October until the eighteenth of February we remained in that camp—drilling, marching, and drilling again. My mother had learned long since, of course, that I was in the army, but though she tried to get me out, she couldn't. How often have I thought since then of the mothers of that awful war—of other awful wars as well. Theirs is the hardest task of all, I know. I didn't know it then, or think so much about it. But what heroism on the field of battle equals the heroism of the mothers who stay at home?

We went in February to Columbus, and then to Cincinnati. There, with orders for service in the South, we went aboard a river steamer, and set sail.

3

ON THE twenty-second of February our regiment disembarked at Paducah, Kentucky, and went into camp about a mile from town. It was here that we were brigaded with the Sixth Iowa and the Fortieth Illinois and were attached to the Fifth Division, commanded by General Sherman.

Being under the command of Sherman pleased me, for while I did not know him, both Father and Mother did. Sherman had, of course, been born in Lancaster, and had gone from there to West Point. Mrs. Sherman, too, had been born there, with the result that my father's brother, Daniel Kyner, who still lived there, knew them very well indeed, while Father and Mother had known them before we moved to the Gilded Swan in Oakland. The Sherman home, too, was still in Lancaster, where Mrs. Sherman's family had long been prominent.

However, a private in the Forty-sixth Ohio got few opportunities to see the divisional commander in those days. I don't even know where he was while we were at Paducah.

It was while we were in this camp that our mules and wagons were issued to us—six mules and one big covered wagon to each company. The herd of mules was in a large corral, six or seven acres in extent, and the men who had been selected from each company to get the company team together went there for them.

Army mules are, of course, notorious creatures, and these particular mules were undoubtedly the very worst of their kind. Many of them, I am sure, had never before had harness on them, with results that were amazing before the next two days were over. Most of the regiment, of course, sensing excitement, crowded about the corral when the unfortunates who had been assigned to the task entered. No rodeo I ever saw in later years equaled that one.

Getting the harness on those mules was most hilarious fun—for those of us outside the fence. I remember one set of fellows who finally got their team all hitched, with the driver on his saddle mule and the jerk line in his hand. Everything had gone with such ease up to that point that it made the men appear either very highly efficient indeed or remarkably lucky. But suddenly those mules were off. The jerk line served to do no more than antagonize them. Within thirty seconds they had started off and wheeled sharply to the right. So short did they turn that the front wheels of the wagon were cramped by the wagon box. And now, seeming to wrap themselves about the wagon, they turned it over, mixed everything all up, and finally threw themselves to the earth, kicking and snorting for those poor fellows to untangle. How it came about that none of the men were hurt I do not know, but we outside the fence thought little enough of that as we clapped our hands and yelled in very glee.

It was a week or so later that we embarked once more, this time for the Tennessee River, where, on March 8, our steamboat made her lines fast at Savannah, Tennessee.

It had been raining heavily for days, and the Tennessee River, a large stream, was filled from bank to bank with swirling water, while we, still crowded aboard our boat, lay there waiting, day after day, for the rest of the army to arrive.

Long before this, because of a song I was forever singing—a song called "The Hamfat Man"—I had been nicknamed "Hamfat," and before we had left Cincinnati, the toughest, hardest specimen of a boy I have ever seen attached himself, quite unofficially, to our outfit. This boy, actually younger than I, I believe, was, so far as the evil ways of the world were concerned, as old as Methuselah. He even *looked* old, his beady little eyes looking out upon the world from a face almost like a monkey's. "Wharf Rat" he had been dubbed, and "Rat," by now, had become his name—the only name I ever knew for him. He chewed tobacco constantly, and had the most uncanny ability to expectorate with fascinating accuracy from either side or from the middle of his mouth.

"Rat," of course, expected little from the world, but there aboard our crowded boat he got rather less than he expected, particularly in the matter of food, and especially in the matter of meat. The supplies from which our regiment was fed left more than a little to be desired, even if one were in a position to choose the best, and "Rat" was never so fortunate as to do that.

One morning, consequently, while we were still awaiting the arrival of the scores of other boats that were on the way with the major portion of the army, "Rat" approached me.

" 'Hamfat,' " he began, "over there on the other side of the river in that canebrake there's a lot o' hogs. I know where there's a nigger dugout, and let's me and you take our guns and git some fresh meat."

The suggestion appealed to me, and having gone to where the dugout was hidden, we paddled it across the river.

I had never been in a canebrake before, and have no desire to enter one again. Nothing in the world but a boy could get about in such a place—a boy or one of those slabsided razorback hogs that lived there. We crashed about among those canes for a time, and finally, at very close range, blasted the life out of one of those hogs with our muskets.

A razorback hog was a new beast to me, and when "Rat" got out his knife in an effort to dissect the animal, I sat down and watched. For an hour I watched "Rat" struggle. The hide on the hog seemed to be made of India rubber, and the hair that grew from it seemed almost to have roots that went inside and wrapped themselves about the bones. "Rat" took "chaw" after "chaw" of tobacco, sweating the while, and finally worked out what he called a ham, though the meat was very tough and fragmentary. However, with this prize, we headed back to where our dugout lay, only to hear, from far downstream, the bands and whistles of the coming fleet.

That dugout canoe was a cranky craft, while the river was wide and filled with rapid waters. Downstream we saw the funnels of numberless ships, and I had never learned to swim in such a river as the Tennessee. Lying flat in the bottom of the dugout, I clutched the bone that "Rat" had called a ham, and wondered if we'd ever get across, or whether we would find ourselves among the scores of thrashing paddle wheels of that tremendous fleet of steamers.

Halfway over I grew disgusted, and consigned that "ham" to the swirling waters. If I had to swim I had no wish to be encumbered with that bone. "Rat" objected when I threw our prize overboard, though he said little, his breath being short because of the work his paddle required of him.

We reached our steamer finally, just as the first of the fleet approached, and there, safe on deck once more, we watched a sight as thrilling as any I have ever seen.

Eighty-seven steamboats crowded with men filled that giant river as far as we could see. Eighty-seven steamboats with bands and calliopes playing, with flags and pennants streaming, with smoke pouring from their funnels, with huge paddle wheels churning the river's swirling waters into foam.

Our own ship cast off her lines, swung out into the stream and took her place in the lead, and from Savannah to beyond Pittsburgh Landing we led the way—an army transported by an inland fleet larger, probably, than any ever previously gathered together in the history of the Mississippi Valley.

Our orders had been to proceed to a point above Pittsburgh Landing, but the country was so flooded that we could not land. We dropped downstream, consequently, to the landing, and there we disembarked, a detail of our regiment being the first of all that army to go ashore.

How long we remained there at the landing I have forgotten, but finally we started on our march to the point where Sherman's division was to be located, going into camp upon the field of what was to become, before so many days had passed, the first really great and sanguinary struggle of the Civil War.

Shiloh Church was a small place for which to name so great a battle, and we, when we went into camp, were almost within sight of that simple little old log church. The logs of which it was built, I remember, had never been squared. They were round and smooth, for they had been peeled, and a single little door gave admittance to its simple interior.

The church stood on the Corinth Road, and Sherman's division, of which we were a part, was encamped off to the west of it a half mile or less, three miles or so from Pittsburgh Landing. The fleet, guarded by two gunboats and a few batteries of siege guns, still lay up and down the river near where we had landed.

Our camp was in an open field, and our division was closest to where the enemy was constantly reconnoitering. It was so obvious that we were exposed and open to attack out there that it was the talk even of the soldiers themselves, while Colonel Worthington of our regiment was constantly insisting, so we were told, that some intrenchments should be erected, or some other defenses prepared. Grant, however, had been left at the little village of Savannah, with orders from Halleck to stay there, and other orders had come from Halleck that nothing in the way of defenses should be prepared. Our colonel, troubled by such a situation, set us to building a corduroy road across a marshy spot near by, and was roundly brought to task for doing so.

A month passed quietly enough. We drilled and marched and were inspected. We cleaned our tents and drilled again, but nothing of consequence occurred that I recall until almost the first of April. Then we became quite conscious of the presence of the enemy. Now and then, by climbing trees, we could see them marching on the distant roads to the west and south. Now and then, too, their pickets came upon our own.

Still, nothing of great consequence occurred until, on April 5, Richard Lee, a member of our company, died of measles. His body, placed in the "dead tent," was guarded by a detail of two men, and Captain Giesy, of our company, assigned Jerome Fields and me to take that duty for the night.

The occasional pop of muskets in the distance had told us plainly that the enemy was near, and after we went on duty at dusk, the firing increased at intervals. Sitting on an empty gun box that lay in front of the tent we listened and talked—talked of many things. From far off through the night would come a little flurry of musket fire now and then, and when it quieted down, Fields would tell me of his life on the Isle of Man, where he was born. He had been in America only two years. Prior to that he had worked for his father who, he said, ran a little traveling show, in which he danced jigs, sang songs, and performed as an acrobat. He was still young, having emigrated to the United States when he had come of age.

The firing now, though no heavier, had come nearer. Occasionally a musket ball would clip through a treetop near by or thud against a trunk. Still it seemed distant, and finally I asked Fields to shift to the end of the gun box, and doubling up my arms, I went to sleep.

I woke in the very early dawn, with the eastern sky ever so faintly gray with the coming of the sun, and the trees near by still black and motionless against the morning sky. I yawned and stretched, sitting up to find Fields still sitting quietly on the end of the gun box, his fine face quiet and very serious.

He looked up at me without a smile, and presently spoke quietly.

" 'Hamfat,' " he said, thoughtfully and seriously,

"we're going to have an awful battle today, and I—I am going to be killed."

He fingered a piece of paper he held, and apparently was going to say more, but I stopped him.

"Aw," I said, "what's the matter with you? We've been on duty all night and we won't have to go out."

"Yes we will," he insisted. "Yes we will."

"But I tell you," I insisted, "we've been on duty and the orderly sergeant will excuse us."

"Now listen," he insisted. "The government's been paying us and training us for months to do a certain thing, and when the time comes to do it, we've got to go."

"But if we're excused," I argued, "it's up to us to stay out of it."

He was obviously not convinced, but by now the long roll was sounding, throbbing through the still and early morning air.

"Listen, 'Hamfat,' " he went on. "I've written a little note here that I want you to give the captain. I have a girl up there at Lancaster and I want her to have my back pay and my land warrant."

I took his note and held it doubtfully.

"But if you get killed," I remarked, "I might, too."

He shook his head.

"No," he replied, with a strange positiveness I have never been able to understand, "you won't."

The musket fire that had been scattering and hesitant was increasing by now, and Fields moved off toward the camp kitchen, so I stuffed his note into my blouse pocket and followed.

As we went down our company street the orderly sergeant was busy getting the men out and properly equipped. They were filling cartridge boxes and cap boxes, or were busy packing their knapsacks and leaving their tents in order.

All of them were hurrying through their preparations when Fields and I stopped at the cook tent for our breakfast, and as we stood there, getting our "dish out," Captain Giesy came out of his tent near by. I watched him as he held his sword belt under his arm and tied the tent flaps. When he had finished, he turned about and, trying to strap his belt about him, came toward us.

He stopped immediately before us, his sword belt caught, and as he straightened it he spoke to us.

"You boys have been on duty all night," he said, "so you remain in camp. And I wish you'd look after the boys' things here and see that nothing is disturbed."

He buckled on his belt and strode off to take command of the company, which now was forming.

"Now there," I remarked to Fields, "the captain has excused us himself, and we don't have to go out."

He shook his head.

"No man," he replied, "can excuse me from doing my duty."

"And you think you're going to be killed, too?" I demanded.

"I know I am," he replied, "and don't you forget to give that note to Captain Giesy."

I had no desire to go out into whatever was going to happen. I was afraid I might get hurt. But if he went, I had to go, and I told him so, as we went to get our guns and take our places in line.

The regiment was formed, and Colonel Worthington, with a group of officers about him, was obviously discussing something important. Presently he took off his uniform blouse and, dismissing the officers about him, turned toward the regiment, holding up both hands.

"We have no regimental colors," he roared, "to rally on. So rally on me today."

We saw, now, why he had dispensed with his blouse. His white shirt was a vivid mark, and we would have little difficulty seeing him among the others, especially as he was on horseback.

There had been, I later learned, a regiment on the left of Sherman's division, that, following a faint-hearted colonel, had precipitately retreated at the very first of the Confederate attack, and we had been ordered to fill the gap. We were marched a little to the rear, where we turned and, following a little road that ran near old Shiloh Church, marched past that simple structure and past a little group of farm buildings that had been Sherman's headquarters. Two hundred yards or so beyond these, we were met by an officer on horseback, and instantly were swung to the right and ordered to lie down.

Just what was going on we had not the slightest idea. That guns were firing we knew well enough, but none, as yet, had appeared in our range of vision. Off to our left the rattle of musketry was continuous by now, but at some distance, though periodically, from far off, the boom of cannon sounded.

We had, however, little time to wonder, for hardly had we lain down in the grass, with a few trees at our rear, than we heard the roar of galloping hoofs, and all in a moment a six-horse team swept past us. A rider rode the nigh horse of each galloping pair, swinging his whip first to the horse beside him and then to the one he rode, while behind them came the heavy caisson and the flashing brass of a twelve-pounder. Down along our front they galloped, and instantly another appeared, followed by another and another.

The sixth of them swung suddenly about immediately before our company. All in a moment that brass twelve-pounder was unlimbered, the caisson in its place, the gunners loading. From where I lay I could see directly between the wheels, beneath the shining barrel, and as I watched, fascinated, I saw the gunner turn the wheel beneath the breech and saw the muzzle rise. He slipped back and raised his hands. Someone pulled the lanyard, and with a roar that great gun fired, almost at the instant that the others in the battery exploded. Vast clouds of smoke burst forth, but to me, lying on the ground, they did not obscure the view. I saw the ball go sailing off through space, straight at one of the farm buildings we had passed only a few minutes before. That anyone was in them we did not know. We had marched past within easy musket range, and no one had fired. But now, with a crash that sent logs and shingles flying, those twelve-pound cannon balls struck. The buildings were hardly two hundred yards away—less perhaps—and we could see them clearly.

The splinters had not settled before a scattering of men ran forth, scurrying to the left. The gunners of the gun before me were already swabbing out the gun. A plume of smoke shot upward from the touchhole. A red flannel bag was thrust into the capacious muzzle and rammed home. Another man stood by with what appeared to me to be a bright tin can, and thrust it in. It too went home.

The men leaped back. The primer was inserted. A

gunner spun the wheel as fast as he could turn it, and as the breech went up the muzzle dropped.

"The fool!" I thought. "He'll shoot into the ground!"

I saw him leap back and raise his hands again. The lanyard jerked. The great gun roared in unison with the others. I watched that shiny can go hurtling off, then fall to the ground, no more than two thirds of the way to where those men were running. But now, strangely enough, the can had burst, and up from where it had struck the ground a fan-shaped cloud of dust and balls were flying. They caught a group of men about the waist. I saw one fellow as he was struck squarely by one of those awful balls, lifted sprawling into the air, and pitched forward on his face.

Twice that battery had fired. Once with solid shot and once with canister. And now the splintered farm buildings were gaping, and the remnants of that broken band were scurrying from sight across a rise.

The horses swung the caissons. The great twelve-pounders were made fast, and off in the direction from which they had come the battery galloped. Who they were I do not know. What else they did at Shiloh I never heard. But they, I know, were gunners.

A sharp command, and we were on our feet. Off to the little road we marched again, down a slope, into a wooded gully. We crossed a bridge, and marching on the outside of the column, I looked over the edge of the little bridge and saw two dead men lying awkwardly in the stream below. Up an incline and to the right we marched, past a field where a group of wounded horses stood, crowding together for comfort. One handsome animal, to which my heart went out, was pushing farther in among the others as I looked, one hind leg shattered and hanging limp. They made no sound. They uttered no complaint. They merely clustered closer for the comfort that it brought. Wounded and cut out of artillery teams, those poor beasts gathered there as we marched past.

A little way beyond, we halted. Before us lay a little valley, through which a creek meandered. Where we had stopped the field was clear, but there before us, filling that depression from bank to bank, the trees stood thick.

"Fix bayonets!" came Captain Giesy's voice.

We pulled them from their leather scabbards, thrust them over the tall muzzles of our guns, and twisted them on.

Off to the left the colonel on his horse, his white shirt bright in the morning sun, was intently watching. Just where the enemy was, he may, perhaps, not quite have known, save that they were ahead. The slope from where we stood down to the stream was free enough of underbrush, with the trees well scattered, but beyond the stream the brush and trees were thick upon the steeper slope that lay there.

The officers gathered in a group about the colonel, and for a moment listened to his orders. Then, suddenly scattering to their places, they stood ready, while the colonel —fine old soldier that he was—raised his hands, and in a voice plain throughout the length of the regiment, gave the only command I heard him give that day.

"Boys!" his great voice boomed across our front. "Follow me!"

Forward we surged, not quite at double-quick, yet rapidly. Over the edge of the field we passed and down the tree-dotted slope. Muskets popped ahead of us somewhere, though not a sign could we see. But suddenly, from fifty feet or so away, a blast of fire burst forth.

Bullets like a storm of hail swept into us. I even saw the bark fly from the trees. Another blast and another, so close that we could feel the heat of them upon our cheeks. The underbrush beyond that stream seemed to erupt with a million streams of fire into our very faces.

I headed for a tree near by and felt a heavy blow upon my side. I staggered and went down, my breath knocked from me, ready to curse the awkward fellow who had struck me so hard, I thought, with the butt of his gun. I struggled to my feet and hurried on a dozen steps perhaps, or less. Still those awful sheets of fire burst from the brush, and now, suddenly, I seemed to stumble. Down I went, and struggled up. Three awkward, staggering steps I made, and fell again, my right leg, below the knee, a crushed and useless thing, spurting blood, crumpled out of shape.

Already that hail of lead was forcing our line back up the slope. They did not run. How well I remember that! I saw a man named Brooks from our company as he passed me, a little distance off. I saw him turn and face the all but invisible enemy, raise his gun and fire. I called to him, but in that storm of sound he did not hear me. Back he went, deliberately, it seemed to me—not hurrying, anyway. And now, no matter where I looked, not one blue uniform could I see, save all about that gentle wooded slope where they were lying on the ground.

I looked at my leg. It was shattered, I knew, beyond repair. My side hurt, too, and when I felt of it, my hand came away red with blood. The tears burst forth; I could not keep them back.

The bullets were less numerous by now, but suddenly I realized that as I sat on the ground, my back was to the enemy. What if a ball should strike me and I should be found with a bullet in my back? I lifted my crushed leg in both hands and struggled about until I faced the other way. What a thing is pride!

The awful firing had stopped by now. The distant sounds of battle still continued, but not that awful, overheated blast from just beyond the stream. My leg, too, was spurting blood—blood that felt like hot water on my hands when I tried to hold it. And now I heard the sound of men advancing. Here and there they appeared in front of me, beside the stream.

The rebels!

I dabbed the tears away with the backs of my bloody hands. No rebel would see me cry, at any rate.

Now they were all about me, some of them moving cautiously up the bank down which, such a little while before, our regiment had come. Most of them, however, stayed there in the hollow—a great crowd, all in civilian clothes, and as I look back now I don't remember seeing a uniform among them, nor an officer that I could recognize as such.

But men were everywhere, and presently I spoke to one who came near. What I said I do not recall, but it was, of course, about my leg, and I know I asked him if he could help me.

He replied that there was a doctor somewhere about, and that he would tell him, whereupon he wandered off, and I wondered whether the doctor would come or not. How long I waited I do not know, but not long, when a man with a little satchel in his hand appeared. He, too, was in civilian clothes, but obviously he was a doctor.

I asked him if he could bandage my leg, and he examined it, shaking his head.

"You'll have to lose it," he remarked, which did not surprise me. I had felt certain that I would.

"Can't you bandage it for me?" I asked.

He patted his pockets.

"All the supplies I have," he said, "are what I have in my pockets and my bag. I'll have to save them for our own men."

His answer disappointed me terribly, I remember, but I agreed with him. It seemed entirely right to me that he should consider his own men first.

"But I'll find a man to help you," he went on.

He walked away, and after awhile a small and elderly man came up. He was unusually short, rather stocky, and wore the most tremendous beard I ever saw on a man so small. There were streaks of gray, I remember, in his beard.

He spoke to me, and seemed to look around for something with which to bind my leg. Finally, finding nothing else, he decided to use a section of my shirt, and drew a gigantic clasp knife from his pocket. He cut a great section from my shirt, tore the hem from it, and wrapping it about my leg, over trousers, underwear and everything, tied it with the hem, and left me.

Long since, the firing had died down. Off in the distance it continued, with the heavy, jarring sound of cannon punctuating it now and then, but the hollow in which I lay was silent now, save for the rebels who were still about, and the groaning of wounded men here and there.

We had charged down into that deadly hollow in the morning, and our men had been driven back at once. How the battle had gone elsewhere I had no means of knowing. How many other deadly hollows there had been I never knew. But that the battle had not ended, was plain all day, for in the distance the faint sound of musketry and the heavy reports of cannon still kept coming to my ears.

4

I LAY on the battlefield of Shiloh from Sunday morning until hours after dark on Monday night. For most of Sunday that bloody little hollow by the stream was quiet enough, with the sounds of battle dimmed by distance. The wave of Confederates had long since passed by me, and the hollow was filled with men who seemed, for the most part, merely to be loitering there. Now and then some fellow would come staggering back with a load of loot upon his back, tied up in an army blanket, perhaps. Here and there along the little stream a campfire burned, with groups of men about, cooking and eating. I fell asleep—or fainted from loss of blood—and lay there for I do not know how long, my head thrown back, my mouth open. When I awoke, my mouth and throat had grown so dry that I could not speak, but I managed, finally, to attract the attention of a man near by, by motioning and pointing to my mouth. He had a pan, I remember, and came at once, dipping water from the stream.

At first the water strangled me, so dry and parched was I, and I distinctly recall his bringing several panfuls, holding my head and trying to help me, and finally I could drink. When he had accomplished that, he called another fellow, and the two of them carried me—I don't know why—across the stream, and put me down beside a tree. On the side where I had fallen a little bank stood two feet high, perhaps, above the water, but now, beside that tree, the bank was low, so low that later that two-foot bank served to shield me from the bullets that swept across.

Evening came and I slept once more, or fainted, and when I awoke the rain was falling on my upturned face. A blanket had been thrown over me—by whom I do not know. But there, among those rebel soldiers in that little hollow I never experienced anything but kindness. They had talked to me occasionally all day, had bound my leg, had given me water, had carried me across the stream, and now, unasked, had given me a blanket. The hatreds of war were far from obvious there among those fellows. They had told me, too, that there among that underbrush their men had been formed five double lines deep—ten lines, each one a little above the line in front. It is no wonder that their fire had seemed so awful in our faces. Blast after blast had swept our regiment back, as line after line had fired.

But now, there in the blackness of the night, the rain was falling heavily, and not a thing could I make out. I felt the blanket—wet and sodden from the rain—and sucked the moisture from its edge occasionally. And then great shells began to fall. They came, I later learned, from the battery of siege guns by the river—great hurtling balls that crashed among the trees. Huge branches, broken by the balls, splintered and creaked and fell, and with the falling of almost every branch some poor devil screamed, so thick were the wounded there among the trees. No shells, thank Heaven, fell very close to me, and all night long I slept—or fainted—and awoke by turns.

I awoke sometime in the morning, and felt a weight upon my chest. Turning my head I saw a young man—hardly more than a boy—lying beside me, holding to my right lapel. I spoke to him, and he answered me, and during the day he told me a little about himself. Someone had carried him to where he lay from somewhere else.

His name was Wallmeier, so he said, and during the day, between those periods of sleep or unconsciousness, I learned that he had been shot directly through the stomach. His back, I think, was broken, but he said not a word of any pain that he was in. Not far off beyond the stream a German, wounded in the knee, lay crying almost constantly: "O Gott! O Gott!" But Wallmeier made no single small complaint.

He knew that he would die. Several men, examining him, told him as kindly as they could that that was true. But even then he offered no complaint. His mother and father, he told me, had felt that every household should do its part to save the Union, and in his home were only his father, his mother, and himself. He had coaxed them, finally, to let him go, instead of having his father, who was a minister, enlist. And now it was of his mother that he thought. That, it seemed, was the only reason he did not want to die. She'd grieve for him, he said—always, always.

All through the hollow the dead and wounded lay. How strangely different were the actions of the wounded! Some groaned. Some sang. One man prayed and swore frightfully by turns, and always that German, thirty feet away, kept up his cry: "O Gott! O Gott!" until I raised myself upon my elbow and swore at him, telling him to stop.

Those great shells from the siege guns kept falling

there on Monday, and once I saw one as it fell up on the slope down which our regiment had come. It bounced in great low leaps like any rubber ball, and came directly for me as I lay there by the stream. It seemed both black and shiny, I remember, and looked as if it might roll to a stop near by. If it did, I thought, I'd like to take it home.

I did not see it stop rolling, for I was suddenly asleep once more. Awakening finally, I felt so microscopically small that I did not know whether or not I was alive. I had no sensation whatever of pain, or even of feeling. I was not even sure I had a body, but finally, opening my eyes, found myself where I had been. Wallmeier was still lying there, but my face and blanket were strewn with twigs and grass and gravel, and there, across the stream, a great hole had been blown in that two-foot bank. I had not been conscious that that great shell had exploded, yet obviously it had, showering us with dirt.

All day the firing had been constant; heavy musketry was forever rattling, and finally the Confederates in that hollow seemed more excited somehow. For so long the place had been a sort of backwater of the battle, but now, from the field that we had marched across, came yells and firing.

The hollow was not an easy place to take. Those within it had the protection of the trees. The attacking force had first to cross that open field. The heavier firing had fairly filled the place with smoke by now—smoke that lay in layers, drifting slowly. By raising my head I could see across the little bank beyond the stream, and following a heavy period of firing, I saw the flag of some Union regiment as it appeared at the top of the rise, just beyond the trees. It wavered there and fell back. Again it came, and disappeared. Once more I saw it, but back it went again.

Five times, it seems to me, those furious charges were beaten back, and then, quite suddenly, a sixth charge came. The rebels ran. They leaped the stream in droves and ran, and in the excitement of what happened I may have been unconscious for a moment, for suddenly the strangest soldier I had ever seen was there above me. He stood behind the tree at the foot of which I lay, and aimed and fired.

I looked him over. Upon his head he had a scarlet fez, from which a yellow tassel fell. He wore a short blue jacket, trimmed with braid, and wore great scarlet bloomers that reached below his knees, while bright white leggins covered his legs. He stood with one foot over me, and fired again.

"What regiment?" I asked, but he did not reply.

I plucked him by those scarlet bloomers.

"What regiment?" I asked again.

He had, I thought, some kind of breech-loading rifle, for his two shots had been fired rapidly. And now, quickly, he looked down at me.

"Woodpeckers from Illinois, by God," he answered, and darted off.

The hollow was now filled with those brilliant uniforms. No formation was apparent. They leaped from tree to tree like Indians, firing as they went, and presently had gone, following the enemy. The rattle of their fire grew fainter as they made their quick advance, and finally the hollow was quieter than it had been before.

I fell asleep again, and woke in the early evening. Wallmeier's hand was on my chest again, and I spoke to him. He did not answer, and I twisted my arm about to feel his face. My fingers touched his cheek, and it was cold.

Night came, so much quieter by now. Again I slept or fainted, and awakening once more, found two men beside me with a lantern. They lifted me to a stretcher, and carried me to an ambulance near by. Then, after awhile, with another fellow they had picked up, they drove across the three miles to Pittsburgh Landing. How that ambulance jolted and jarred. I do not recall their lifting me out, but finally I awoke again to find myself upon the ground beside the log house that was the only structure at Pittsburgh Landing.

The place at which I lay was sloping, and a road ran beside me. Someone, thinking apparently to keep me from rolling to the road where horses and wagons were forever passing, had put a rail beside me. And there I lay, quite unattended until midafternoon of the next day. It was, I felt, even more uncomfortable than the place at which the men with the ambulance had found me.

But finally two men came up and put me on a stretcher. They lifted me and took me into that log house, and put me down among some others who were wounded. For a time I lay there—long enough to learn that the structure was in reality two log houses with a roofed porch between.

They came for me again, and one of the two nodded his head sidewise at a man lying close beside me.

"Dead," he said to the man he was assisting, and without another word they carried me out to the porch and lifted me to an operating table.

It seems strange to me now that I recall so much of the surroundings of that place. A large and heavy man stood at the foot of the table, and I sat up. Across the porch rail, a dozen feet away, I saw a heap of legs and arms and nameless, shapeless things that reached a little higher than the rail. A helper stepped up with a chloroform-soaked sponge and put his hand upon my chest to push me down. But first I wanted to talk to that surgeon. I knew I'd have to lose my leg, but I wanted to keep as much of it as possible. The fellow pushed again, and I cursed him; I used a torrent of army language that fairly sparkled.

The doctor laughed.

"Let him alone," he ordered, and the fellow dropped his hand.

I talked rapidly, and told him not to cut off any more than was absolutely necessary. The wound was six inches or so below the knee, and all of that I wanted saved.

The doctor nodded.

"That's good surgery," he replied. "That's good surgery. I'll do it."

"On your honor," I demanded, "as a surgeon and a gentleman?"

"On my honor as a surgeon and a gentleman," he nodded. "Now, young man, keep a stiff upper lip and you'll come out all right."

I lay down, and instantly that great chloroform sponge came down upon my face. I struggled, tried to get my breath; and then I went under, knowing nothing, hearing nothing save a steady "tick-tick-tick," perhaps of a watch or a clock near by.

When I awoke it was early dusk, and I was on the stretcher once again, back in the room from which they had taken me. For a moment I lay befogged, and then remembered. But had the surgeon kept his word? I reached down and felt my bandaged leg. There it was—a great bandaged bundle below my knee. Satisfied, I drew a long breath and went to sleep.

The next I knew two men were carrying my stretcher down the path to a steamer that lay there against the river bank. I saw her name in giant letters on her paddle box—the *J. J. Roe*. But as we approached the gangplank an officer barred our path, insisting that the ship was already so overloaded that his crew could not work.

The two who carried me told him that if he'd let them put me aboard they would bring no more, and finally he agreed. Across the gangplank they took me, and up to the hurricane deck, where they set me down—stretcher and all, beside a funnel. All about were wounded men, but they were lying on the deck. I had my stretcher.

I lay there for awhile and presently felt a hand upon my shoulder. Looking up, I recognized Sol Homan, who came from Lancaster. His left hand was off at the wrist, but he was bright enough, strolling about with his arm bound up across his chest. He asked me a few questions and disappeared, returning presently with the colonel of our regiment.

The lights by now were lighted—great metal baskets hung on brackets and filled with fat pine sticks. They hung out over the water on each side of the gangplank, and one hung outside the rail there on our deck. The colonel, with a notebook in his hand, asked questions of me—my name, my company, where I had been wounded. He wrote something in his little book.

"By God, Kyner," he said. "I'll reward you."

And off he went along the deck in search of others of his regiment.

Sol Homan disappeared again, and after a time came

back with Captain Giesy. I was glad to see the captain, and after I had answered a question or two of his, I asked one of my own.

"Was our company hurt much, Captain?"

"Jimmy," he replied, and his face was serious, "only thirteen answered at roll call this morning."

"Did Fields answer?" I demanded.

"No," he said slowly, "Fields was killed out there where you were shot."

"Well, he *said* he was going to be killed," I cried, "and he gave me a note to give to you."

I reached into my blouse pocket and drew it forth. It was stained, I saw, but whether by blood or not I do not know. He took it and unfolded it carefully—read it slowly. I watched him as he read, and saw tears in his eyes as he stood there. He reached into the tail pocket of his coat and drew out a handkerchief, and a tear dropped down upon my face. He stooped over and wiped my cheek before wiping his own eyes, and then, stooping again, put his hand upon my forehead.

"Jimmy," he said, "I hope you get home all right."

He turned and left, disappearing about the wheelhouse.

General Halleck arrived from St. Louis that evening, and some idiot ordered a salute fired by those awful cannon. Every wounded man aboard that boat was shaken and rocked and hurt by the heavy concussions. All about, the men were cursing—cursing Halleck. No cheering greeted him. Only curses from the wounded men, whose wounds were so largely due to Halleck's inane orders that there be no earthworks built.

The ship cast off her lines a little later, and I slept.

When I awoke it was still night, and the ship had stopped. I asked someone who passed me why.

"Carrying off some dead men," he replied, and went on his way.

We did not stop again, if I remember correctly, until the next day, and then it was to land some wounded somewhere. Then, in the afternoon, we came to Evansville, where I awoke to find myself ashore, the steamer far away at the river bank, and a great brick building not far off. They carried me to that building, and I remember them starting with me up some stairs, but then I passed out again, and the next I knew I was in a low cot—bathed—my hair cut—my filthy clothes taken from me, and a white cotton nightshirt on.

The room I was in was perhaps eighteen or twenty feet square, with ten or a dozen wounded men in cots. A German whom I later learned to call Marty was the nurse in charge, and despite his strictness, or perhaps because of it, he was excellent. We were the first wounded to arrive in Evansville from Shiloh, and the battle having been ended only two days before, the town was a seething mass of excitement. Our room, however, under Marty's strict rule, was quiet enough. I remember that one of the men died the next day, just before his mother and his sister arrived. They were brought to the room all unprepared, perhaps, for such a tragedy, and the moment they saw him lying dead they both cried out.

Old Marty rushed at them, and growled his orders for silence, thrusting them into the hall. There were some among us, he knew, who could stand no scenes like that.

People came in droves to the hospital. Gifts and more gifts came to all of us. Oranges, candy, and I forget what else were lined along both sides of my low cot. Women and girls were always coming and going, and one family —Mrs. Lister with a married daughter and another about seventeen—seemed to adopt me. How kind they were!

It was not long after they began to come that I, boylike, feeling of my wound, pulled two threads from it, and dropped them on the floor. Old Marty came by presently, and stopping there, looked at them.

"Vat de Hell is diss?" he asked.

I told him.

"D' Hell," he muttered. "D' Hell," and left to bring the doctor.

Quietly the doctor looked me over.

"Young man," he ordered finally, "you lie quietly there."

And Marty, knowing well what I had done, was stricter than ever, and kept that room in almost perfect silence. It was then, I learned later, that Mrs. Lister telegraphed my mother.

It was, I suppose, the second day thereafter that Mrs. Lister came in and, kneeling down beside that low cot, began to talk to me.

"I suppose you'd like to see your mother," she said.

I naturally agreed.

"Well," she went on. "You know you're in rather delicate condition. If your mother happened to come in, what would you do?"

I had no suspicions.

"You wouldn't try to sit up, would you?"

I said I wouldn't. But she cautioned me, and talked on for awhile, finally putting her hand upon my forehead.

"Well," she said finally, "if you'll be real quiet, I'll bring your mother in."

I started, naturally.

"There, there," she cautioned. "Keep quiet."

And when I had recovered a little composure, she went out. How I watched the door! How I waited!

The door opened, presently, and Mother entered, with Mrs. Lister and another woman at her side. I can see her clearly in her poke bonnet and her shawl. She came to me at once, dropping down beside me. She put her arms about me, and all she said at first was just: "My boy! My boy!"

Two days later, Mrs. Lister, having obtained the permission of the surgeon in charge, had me taken to her home. What a change! There I lay in a great bright bedroom, with Mother constantly attending to my needs, with Mrs. Lister and her daughters thoughtful of every comfort. By now, although hardly more than a week had passed since the battle, I was demanding crutches. And those good-hearted people, doing everything to humor me, bought me a pair.

But Mother—poor Mother. She had left the tavern to the care of my eldest sister, who was fourteen. As yet Father had not returned from California, and Oakland, already hurt by the near-by towns, was ruined by the war. The tavern produced an income pitifully small, and there were five children there, from two to fourteen. That Mother was needed there was no doubt, but when she spoke of going I would not hear of it, unless I went as well.

And so we went. Taken to the train in Mrs. Lister's carriage, we met nothing but kindness on the way. The hostess of the hotel in Cincinnati where we spent the night would take not a cent in payment. A brigadier general, at Morrow, where we had to change cars, carried me from one train to the other. Glancing down, as he held me in his arms, I saw the single star of his rank upon his shoulder strap.

I almost laughed.

"It isn't often," I said as he held me, "that a private finds himself in the arms of a brigadier."

"No," he admitted. "No. I hope it will do you some good."

At Circleville, where we had expected to have John Erie take us in his stage, the local Sanitary Commission unit (the Red Cross of the Civil War) insisted that we let them take us in a carriage. But John was not to be outdone. Despite the fact that his route took him farther on the way to the Gilded Swan, he poured the leather into his horses to such effect that he reached Lancaster ahead of us. They told me afterward about it.

Along the pike the stage came galloping, and as it reached the town, John started shouting.

"Jim Kyner's comin'!" he roared out. "Jim Kyner's comin'!"

And long before his stage had stopped, the quiet, almost deserted little town was excitedly gathering. Our carriage came in a little later, while there on the tavern porch and in the street the crowd had gathered.

George Calahan, his stiff red beard bristling in his excitement, came elbowing through the crowd.

"I'm going to carry him!" he shouted. "I'm going to carry him in."

Never was a baby carried more gently than George carried me, and fourteen days after I had gone with my company into that bloody hollow at Shiloh I was home. I received my discharge from the army, too, before my wound was healed, and months before my sixteenth birthday my first enlistment in the army had come to an end.

Oakland had changed, and the Gilded Swan had changed. Where formerly the town had bustled about the inn each evening when the stage arrived, now the place was almost deserted, with only a quiet little group about. Folks from all about came in to see me. Presents came every day from somewhere. But the present I recall most clearly was a great red apple, brought by Naomi Conrad, who was ten years old.

She came into the room shyly, her pink cheeks pinker for her excitement, and she did not come close to the bed. She stood, instead, a little distance off, and leaning far over, held the apple out. How often I have thought of that, for fourteen years later she and I were married.

How poor we were in those days, with prices going up and up, and the trade of the Gilded Swan all but gone. Father's trip to California had not brought him much. He had sent a little from time to time, and now he returned with something, it is true, but not with much. And Mother, her cares multiplied by my return, must have been heavily taxed. Uncle Dan Kyner and Aunt Jane, who lived in Lancaster, coming down to Oakland, suggested that they take me, and so to Lancaster I went. I was much better now, of course, and shortly after I was established in the comfortable old house in Broad Street, Mrs. William Tecumseh Sherman, with her coachman and her carriage, came and took me for a ride. I was on the porch, I remember, when that wonderful woman, the wife of one of America's great soldiers, arrived, and as she approached me she said a little prayer.

For two years I remained in Lancaster, and when I

was going about on crutches the father of the boy who had died beside me on the battlefield came there, to have me tell him all that tragic story. I've rarely seen such suffering as was on his face, yet he insisted on hearing every painful fact.

By 1863 I had an artificial leg, and learning from "Lash" Hall that the government was reënlisting convalescents in the Reserve Corps—called by some the Invalid Corps—I enlisted again, this time in the 111th Company of the Second Battalion. I was made a corporal, and for some reason I never knew, or have forgotten, was given a straight sword in a leather scabbard as a mark of my high office. Under a Lieutenant Black I went to Dayton on recruiting service for a time, and then was sent to Columbus.

While I was on this duty the election of 1864 came on, and every man whose home was near enough was given leave in order that he might cast his vote. I was only eighteen, of course, but I got my furlough with the others, and in company with "Lash" Hall, went to Lancaster.

I had no intention of voting, but when I went with "Lash" up to the polling place, two ballots were handed out, of which "Lash" handed one to me. The watcher at the poll knew both of us, and knew as well as I how old I was. He called Hall's name, and "Lash" marked his ballot, handing it over to have it dropped into the ballot box. He then, to my surprise, called out my name, and I, thinking that he was merely flattering my vanity, marked the ballot with a flourish and handed it over.

To my amazement the fellow dropped it in the ballot box.

"Good Lord," I whispered to "Lash." "He put it in."

"You better watch out," replied Lash, his eyes big with surprise. "Some of these Democrats'll put you in jail for illegal voting."

We hurried away from the poll, and I was afraid. I could almost feel some Democratic watcher at my heels. It bothered me so much, in fact, that though I had two days more on my leave, I went back to Columbus and reported. The watcher has still to put me in jail for that offense, and it has been some time since it has worried me. As a matter of fact, I have some pride in having cast that vote for Lincoln.

Until late in 1864 I remained in the Invalid Corps, and finally, having no duties of importance, I asked for my discharge. The war was obviously approaching its end. The great final campaign was not far off, and I, eighteen, with an education far from complete—with one leg gone—with a father who by now had been for two years in uniform—with a mother struggling to live and to keep that family together—had a future of my own of which I had to think.

5

FOR YEARS after the Civil War, conditions in the United States, so far as I knew them, were so infinitely worse than any I have ever seen since as to make it difficult to tell the story of those times to later generations. I finished high school, but would never have been able to attend college if it had not been for the generosity of Darius Tallmadge. He was an old friend of our family, and his father, it is interesting to note, for it shows how young our country is, had been a colonel in the Revolutionary War. At Mr. Tallmadge's suggestion and at his expense I attended Ohio University at Athens for three years. My roommate was Luke Clark, a nephew of General Sherman, and together we played the pranks that college boys have always played, and learned this and that, though I can't remember now just what it was.

Horace Greeley, in those days, was busily engaged with his "Go West, young man," and the building of the Union Pacific Railroad was keeping news of the West constantly before us. I grew restless consequently, and thinking, as so many youngsters have thought before and since, that I knew enough to see me through life, left school and went to Illinois.

In Logan County, in and about the village of Mt. Pulaski, were many people who had gone there from

Lancaster and Oakland, some of them our relatives, and so to Mt. Pulaski I went. For two years I taught school, a part of the time at sixty dollars a month, which was a munificent salary for the time. My remuneration was set at that high figure when I consented to teach in a school from which two teachers had been driven away by the toughness of the older boys. I had no especial trouble, for having soundly thrashed one ornery boy of fourteen, and having run his grown brother out of the schoolyard when he came to punish me, order began to prevail.

I boarded with one George Shupe, where breakfast, I remember, was invariably of mush and milk. Not once was any other dish served at breakfast in that house all the time that I was there.

It was common, in those days, for such schools as mine to have evening gatherings made up of pupils and former pupils, together with any others who cared to come, at which we entertained ourselves with "spelldowns." These were called "spelling schools," but the rough young men in the vicinity had so often ruined these erudite occasions that they had not been held for months. I decided, however, to begin them again, and at the first one, which was well attended, three young men appeared, one of whom, a little unsteady from too much whiskey, rose in the midst of the affair, and planting his feet wide apart as he stood before me, shook his fist in my face.

"Hell's fire!" he bawled. "This ain't no spellin' school!"

I leaped to my feet and went for him. Another fellow told me afterward that I leaped clear off the floor as I struck the shouting fool. But whether I did or not, he went down like a felled ox, and seizing him by the collar, I dragged him to the door and rolled him down the steps into the bitter cold outside. From then on our "spelling schools" were polite affairs.

The Gilded Swan, in Oakland, had been sold by now —the furnishings auctioned off—and our family, with little of this world's goods, had come to Macon County, Illinois, where Father rented a farm from Dr. David Kyner, a cousin and a practising physician of Macon. The farm was excellent, and the prairie chickens and other birds were thick upon it—too thick, we thought, for crops were difficult to raise when literally millions of those handsome fowls had first to get their livelihood from the fields. Great bands of whooping cranes, too, were about, flapping their wings and dancing in circles as they whooped. It was often difficult to sleep in the very early mornings, because of the sounds of the cranes and prairie chickens.

In Decatur, from which the farm was only twelve or fifteen miles distant, lived several relatives. Among them was Uncle Dick Oglesby, then Governor of Illinois, and later United States Senator. As a matter of fact, from 1865 to 1889 Uncle Dick played a prominent part in Illinois politics, serving as governor three different times. He was a handsome, delightful old fellow—a bachelor—who had been a colonel in the war. He had been a rather heroic officer, and had an ounce ball in his lung, to prove that he had smelled powder smoke. Some said that it took that ounce of lead to make him governor, though they, I suspect, were somewhat less his friends than they might have been. He had, it is true, been something of a popular hero as a soldier, and no doubt that served to make him politically popular as well. He was a highly successful attorney, a friend of Abraham Lincoln, and, naturally, had been a political supporter of Lincoln as well. And now Uncle Dick persuaded me to study law in the unusually complete law library that he owned, and in which he never opened a book.

I tackled it, but those endless pages wore my patience out. The West was still my major interest, and in the winter of 1869-70, I set out. An eclipse of the sun in December, 1869, was enough to keep me in Decatur until it was over, but immediately after New Year's I bought my ticket and began my journey west to Hannibal, Missouri; from there to St. Joseph, where the pony express had formerly had its eastern terminus; and finally to Council Bluffs, Iowa.

It was for a little mill on a branch of the Elkhorn River in Nebraska that I was heading, for John Olney, whom I had known in Decatur, had gone there to help Colonel Mathewson, his father-in-law, complete the mill and get it to operating. John had written me of the wonderful land in the little valley, where I could take up a claim of one hundred and sixty acres and become a landholder in the West, as Horace Greeley was urging young men like me to do.

The train from St. Joseph to Council Bluffs ran all night, I remember, and finally backed down along a siding among the sand and willow clumps beside the Missouri River. There was no bridge there then, of course, and the river, being frozen, had tied up the ferry. Furthermore, the ice was hardly thick enough for the bus to drive across, so those of us bound for Omaha, on the farther bank, had to walk.

Some, I remember, with ropes tied to their trunks, skidded them across the ice, where planks were laid here and there to help us across the weaker places. I had no trunk, and toted my valise across that wide and slippery expanse of the Missouri River, to where the half-dead town of Omaha stood among the clay banks and bluffs of the farther side.

During all the building of the Union Pacific, Omaha had been a thriving, hustling place. But the railroad had been completed the year before, and the town had staggered in its stride. Fully half of the buildings of the community were empty. Here and there the wooden sidewalks had sunk into the mud, or planks were missing, making it more than risky enough to walk about them in the dark.

The depot was a cheap wooden building, in the bare waiting room of which a great round cast-iron stove, heated in places to a cherry red, threw out heat enough to warm the place. Few people were in the waiting room, seated uncomfortably on the bare benches.

Columbus, ninety miles from Omaha, was where I had been told to go, for there, John Olney had written me, Elias Shook, who drove the supply wagon for the mill company, would be. I had no desire to miss him, for the mill lay forty-two miles from Columbus—quite a walk for January in Nebraska.

I asked the time of the first train out, consequently, and paid nine dollars—ten cents a mile—for my ticket to Columbus. Later I was to ride thousands of miles back and forth, throughout the length of the Union Pacific, all on annual passes, but certainly I paid enough for that first ride along its wavy rails.

I suspect that none of the Union Pacific rolling stock was new. Certainly the passenger trains were not. The one I took to Columbus on that January day in 1870 was made up of cars that had been bought from the Pennsylvania Railroad, and was drawn by an old locomotive that had burned wood back east, but here in this almost treeless land was burning coal.

The coaches were somewhat inelegantly described as "sow-belly cars," because of the structure of their underbodies, and less attractive contraptions have never been designed. The windows were about ten by twelve inches in size—so small that from the outside they were hardly noticeable, while from the inside one had to stretch one's neck considerably to look through them at all. The cars were lighted by candles—huge candles, an inch and a half or thereabouts in diameter—and a patent arrangement kept their flames always at the same level within the globe of glass that surrounded them.

The cars were coupled together by links and pins, and the road itself, which had been laid for the most part directly on the prairie sod, undulated up and down across those prairie irregularities without the benefit of cuts or fills save where cuts and fills were vital. Because of the links that joined the cars, the last car was not moving until the locomotive had taken up the slack all along the train, nor did it stop until an appreciable time after the locomotive had come to rest. A train of ten cars would be ten feet or so longer when it was starting than when it was coming to a stop, and the same difference was obvious when the grade was up and when it happened to be down.

To me, consequently, the ride to Columbus was a constant teetering upon my seat, swaying from side to side and jolting back when the track was climbing one of those gentle prairie swells, jerking forward when the car, over the top, coasted and rattled down upon the cars ahead. There were few passengers, however, and when the worn cushions of one seat grew too uncomfortable, I shifted to another. There may have been a comfortable seat in that car, but I had not found it by the time we reached Columbus.

Columbus was a small cluster of buildings, yet it had been a place of some importance for years, owing to the fact that a portion of the Oregon Trail that came from St. Joseph forded the Platte River there. The trail was no longer so important as it had been, of course, for the railroad now went to the coast, but for years one of the most amazing movements in all the development of America had passed through Columbus, and more than a few covered wagons were still using the historic old route.

It was early evening when I dropped off the train, only to find, to my vast disappointment, that 'Lias Shook had already left. Inquiry at the Clothier House—the hotel of the place—elicited the information that Shook always drove in the evening to the Tracy Creek Ranch, ten miles away, in order the more readily to drive the remaining thirty-two miles to the mill on the following day.

As I ate my belated supper I asked how I could get to the Tracy Creek Ranch that night, and old man Clothier, the proprietor, going to the window, looked out and came back with the announcement that a blizzard was coming. I can see him yet, as he stood there talking. He hadn't a tooth left in his head, and his wrinkled old jaw was clamped down on the butt of a cigar until it looked as if his head had been squeezed flat in a cider press. His son, however, said that he would take me for a consideration. I asked him how much, and he replied that he wouldn't do it for less than five dollars.

I had no idea when 'Lias Shook would come to Columbus again, and though five dollars was most of what I had, I agreed. Once I reached the mill it mattered little whether or not I had any money at all.

We started off into the night in a light spring wagon, and within ten minutes that blizzard was upon us, whistling out of the northwest, blowing the snow in almost level lines across the prairie, so thick, at times, that we could not make out our horses' heads.

Two hours or more on that bare, exposed, uncomfortable wagon seat did little enough to warm us up, and when we drove up before the door of the Tracy Creek Ranch house, I was glad enough to open the door and step in unannounced.

'Lias Shook was there, thank goodness, and the house was warm and comfortable enough. The logs of which it was built must have been hauled for many a long mile, but they had been welded into a fairly weatherproof house, the chinks plastered with mud, the floor merely of earth, and the furniture simple enough. There was only one room, with a lean-to, and a floored attic. But seven of us, if I remember correctly, spent the night there. 'Lias, owing to the fact that he was a regular visitor, had a bed in the attic, but I, with two young fellows bound for a claim they had near Madison, had to sleep upon the attic floor, while the man who owned the place, together with his wife and baby, occupied the room downstairs.

It was a bit cold for the two young fellows with whom I slept, but not for me. Seeing that I had lost a leg, they generously offered me the place in the middle, and then the two of them, finding the blankets somewhat narrow to cover all of us and tuck in against the floor, waged an alternating tug of war, the results of which were always bad for one or the other of them, but never once for me.

Shook and I started off in the morning, with the blizzard over and the prairie blown mostly clear of the snow that had fallen, and by suppertime had halted before the little store that stood beside the partially built mill, there on the north bank of the Elkhorn River.

A mill, not quite completed, a store, two houses, and a blacksmith shop made up the community. Not long before, the place had been named Norfolk, and today is as nice a town as one is likely to find in all that prairie country. Then, however, it left something to be desired.

Colonel Mathewson, who came from Pomfret, Connecticut, and had been the government agent at the Winnebago Indian Agency, had built the mill, and had erected, as well, a house that was quite the most pretentious in all that portion of Nebraska—a house of two stories and eight rooms, weatherboarded and, compared with other houses, vast.

It was here I stayed for a time. Finally, however, we built a school two miles or so away, and then, having been chosen as teacher, I went to live with old Tim Carabine, whose claim lay beside the Elkhorn River. I took up a claim, too, on a little creek we called the Spring Branch, and sent for Father to come as well.

It was in the summer of 1870 that I saw, camped across the river from Tim Carabine's place, three thousand Ponca Indians out on the last great buffalo hunt that took place in Nebraska. The tepees covered so huge a stretch of ground as to make it impossible for me to estimate them. Men, women, children, horses, dogs were there in endless confusion. It was by far the largest band of Indians I ever saw. The tepees were, I remember, mostly, if not entirely, of canvas, and the clothes that the Indians were wearing were mostly of trade cloth. The braves, of course, wore nothing but their breech clouts and their moccasins. Here and there a little buckskin was in evidence, but not much, their clothes of beaded leather being put aside for the time being. For several days they camped there, finally moving on—the last time that any such movement ever took place in Nebraska.

I built a slab shack on my claim that fall, and Father arrived before Christmas, having driven a wagon and two teams from Illinois with my brother Dan, a boy of thirteen. There was a little three-room house in Norfolk in addition to the colonel's "mansion," and this we took. In the following April, Mother and my sisters Jane and Nancy Ann came by train to Council Bluffs, where Father met them. Three days later, almost frozen in a blizzard that had blown for hours into their very faces, they drove into Norfolk to begin a period of difficulties that made our earlier vicissitudes look mild enough.

We built a two-story, four-room house upon my claim, and went to work. The house was not finished when we moved in in the fall of 1871, and cold weather came down on us before we could complete it. Our breath often froze our sheets and pillowcases about our faces. Once, I remember, a wisp of my sister Jane's hair was frozen to her pillow, where all night the moisture from her breath had been condensed upon it.

There were many Indians in the country, of course, but the region about Norfolk was never the scene of Indian trouble. They often came into the town, and on one occasion I saw a squaw paring down a hide in the street before the mill company's store, preparatory to tanning it. It interested me to see that she felt for the inequalities of the skin with her bare feet as she stood stooped over and scraped it down.

On another occasion an Indian came up to our house and asked if he could have a chicken. He had a bow slung over his shoulder, and wondering just how accurate such a fellow might be with his arrows, I told him he could have one if he would shoot it with his bow and arrow.

He drew his bow over his shoulder and strung it in a flash, pulled an arrow from his quiver, notched it, and let fly at a chicken twenty feet or so away. No one could have unslung a gun and fired more quickly. Nor could a gun have been more accurate, for the arrow went squarely through the chicken's head.

The Indian troubles of earlier days were largely over, but still, more than a few difficulties were to arise throughout the West, and scalps were still being taken occasionally. That no such difficulty arose about Norfolk was merely our good fortune, for near-by counties saw scalping knives at work now and then.

Not long after I arrived at Norfolk a party of us decided to go on a hunting trip. Colonel Mathewson and his son Charles, John McClarey, Louis Sessions, and I made up the group, and with two saddle horses, a team and a wagon we started off. We made a circuitous trip through Antelope County, finally pitching our tent beside a little stream called the Dismal River in what is now Boone County.

The day we pitched camp there we had supper early —a supper of venison and flapjacks—and I was busy over the campfire, somewhat proud of my ability to throw the flapjacks into the air, turn them over, and catch them in the frying pan again. It takes a lot of flapjacks, you can be sure, to feed five hungry men, and my back grew tired. I straightened up to rest it.

Downstream and across it we could see for miles. The prairie, of course, was without a single tree, and even along the stream the trees were few. But as I stared off across the little river and the prairie I saw what appeared to be game.

"Look over there," I called out. "There's some elk."

They all looked up, and Charlie Mathewson rose to his feet.

"Doesn't look like game to me," he remarked, and went into the tent to get his father's spyglass.

In another moment he was out and had the old glass focussed.

"It's Indians," he explained, "but it's only a small party. On a hunt, I suppose."

But as we watched more Indians appeared, and more, and within a few minutes it began to look as if an army was out there on the prairie.

Charlie still had the spyglass, and I was glad that he and his father were with us. Colonel Mathewson had been a very successful Indian agent for years, and Charlie had lived among the Indians, as well, and knew them.

"A party is coming this way," remarked Charlie. "Six of them."

We watched them as they trotted their horses toward the ford which lay some hundreds of yards downstream. The main band had stopped while the half-dozen horsemen obviously were being sent ahead to have a powwow.

"Better go to meet them, Charlie," suggested the Colonel.

Charlie did not reply, but got his gun, and mounting his saddle horse rode off with the gun across his lap. Fifty yards or so from camp he pulled up his horse, and as the Indians approached him he put up his hand with the palm toward them. They stopped at once, whereupon he put up one finger and beckoned. One Indian advanced, and for a time the two talked in sign language, with a little Winnebago, an Indian language that Charlie knew well.

After a time the other five were called up, and all of them came with Charlie back to camp. The main party now rode down to the ford and crossed the river, and the six ambassadors went back to meet them, bringing the whole party, of whom there were over a hundred, back toward us in a greatly extended and very neatly aligned "company front."

A hundred Indians may not sound very formidable, but they certainly *looked* formidable to me. They were Sioux—all fine specimens, magnificently mounted. And that this was a war party was perfectly obvious by now.

The leader was a little in advance of the extended line of horsemen, and by his side rode a squaw—the only woman with them. I learned later that a squaw was often taken by such parties to bring success and good luck. She was dressed in a blue skirt and a blue shirt. Her hair was parted and braided, while the part was painted bright red. She wore beaded moccasins, and was dressed as if for a party.

There was not, I remember, a bridle on one of those horses. Each animal had a line looped over his lower jaw, and every Indian was riding bareback. They rode toward us at a walk, and as they approached they began to blow whistles and shout. The beads on their leggins glistened in the late sunlight. Bands of brass and silver glinted on their arms. Other metal decorations hung at their breasts, flashing as they moved, and making a very imposing picture.

They stopped a few yards away, and thirty or forty of them dismounted, while one of the men who had been in the advance guard took Colonel Mathewson to the chief. The Winnebagos and the Sioux were on good terms, and some among these visitors of ours recognized the Colonel from having seen him when he had been in charge of the Winnebago Agency.

Two men who had ridden near the center of the extended line had been carrying tall poles from which something was dangling surrounded by red flannel streamers. Wondering what these signified, I approached and looked at them. One of the men, seeing that I was interested, proudly lowered his pole until the dangling thing was directly before my eyes. To my amazement I saw that it was a scalp—a fresh scalp, too, and another dangled from the other pole. The hair of these scalps was eight or nine inches long, but the flesh that had been cut from the scalped men was hardly larger than a silver dollar.

Colonel Mathewson and Charlie, meanwhile, were busy talking in a mixture of Sioux, Winnebago, and sign language, and were being told that those two mementos on the poles were Pawnee scalps, taken early that morning. Furthermore, the Indians assured us that a tremendous body of angry Pawnees were even then upon their trail, bent on vengeance. They warned Colonel Mathewson, in sign language, that if we remained where we were we stood an excellent chance of having our throats cut, and they advised us to move both rapidly and far.

We moved, too, loading our camp equipment into our wagon and heading back the way we had come, nor did we camp until very, very late that night.

For some reason or other one of the Indians stuck a couple of arrows into the meat we were eating when they arrived, and I still have one of those arrows.

We settlers about Norfolk were fortunate, of course, in having no trouble with the Indians, but it must not be thought that our other troubles were not serious. In 1871 and 1872 we got fair crops, but crops were one thing and prices were another. I hauled wheat across the forty-two miles to Columbus and sold it there at thirty cents a bushel. I sold four thousand bushels of corn, which Father and I had husked largely by moonlight, and was paid ten cents a bushel when we had put it in August Pilger's crib.

By July, 1873, however, we had a field of corn of which we were very proud indeed. It was tall and strong and early, and bid fair to produce a crop so large that we would make a little, even at the low price we were almost certain to get. I went to town the day I have in mind, and noticed as I started home that the sunlight was growing hazy. I thought little of it, however, and having forded the river, drove along fairly pleased with our prospects. What my mind was on I do not know, but I saw nothing coming, when suddenly the grasshoppers were about me in such infinite numbers as to seem impossible. They flew into the horses' faces until the poor beasts backed and tried to turn around. They actually hurt me as they flew against my face and hands. The wagon I was driving was literally filled with them. The road was seething; the grass along the way was hidden. The horses' hoofs crushed scores of them at every step. The wagon wheels sounded as if they were running over popcorn.

I struggled with the horses every step of the way home, and when I got there I saw Father standing almost in despair. So thick were the grasshoppers in the corn-field of which both of us had been so proud, that not a spot of green could be seen. And within two hours of the time that they had come not a leaf was left in all that field. The stalks that still were left were merely ragged stumps, and where many a stalk had stood, a hole in the ground was all that remained—a hole where the grasshoppers had eaten the stalk off an inch or more below the ground.

Our wheat, too, was ruined, for though it was too ripe for them to eat, they cut almost every head from the stalks. We salvaged some of that, it is true, but the corn was utterly, completely gone.

I was drawing a pension for my wound at Shiloh—a pension of eight dollars a month, paid twice a year. How fortunate that was! Without that forty-eight dollars coming twice a year I do not know what would have happened to us. There were many in the country 'round about who had no such anchor to windward, and settlers heading back toward where relatives lived in the states farther east were common enough. They took it good-naturedly, it is true, and painted humorous signs on their wagons, but it was more than serious enough.

"Going home to Mother," read one sign on a wagon. "Going east to my wife's folks," read another. These were common sights in the seventies in Nebraska.

In 1874 and 1875 the grasshoppers came again—less destructively, but destructively enough. Furthermore, the prices still were low. My ambition to be a farmer and a landowner in the West waned. In the late autumn of 1875, therefore, I went back to Ohio and ultimately, with Hamilton Rockey, who had married Uncle Dan Kyner's daughter Cordelia, I went into the insurance business. We did reasonably well from the first.

On January 20, 1876, I was married to Naomi Conrad who, fourteen years before, had come, a little girl of ten, to give me a red apple when I reached home from Shiloh.

I had been to New York just before our wedding, to get a new artificial leg, but about all I had when we were married was my nerve and that new wooden leg.

For nearly three years we remained in Lancaster and in Oakland, the insurance business doing fairly well. A son, whom we named Tallmadge, was born in '77. Another son, named Gordon, was born in '78, and later that year, having obtained the Nebraska agency for an insurance company, we moved to Omaha.

For fourteen years things had gone quite slowly enough, but now the tempo quickened. The worst of the postwar depression had been passed. The future was brightening, and by good luck I went, in my travels about the state of Nebraska, to David City, in Butler County, at a time when the local people were opposing some railroad enterprise that had been proposed.

Just how it happened that I was asked to speak I do not know, but ultimately I was. Why those people failed so utterly to see the vital need of railroads I never understood, and I talked to them seriously. I told them that a land could be settled by covered wagons, but could not be developed by such means. I told them more things, too, and ended by insisting that it was in the interest of every farmer that a railroad should reach every county.

Having done my talking I more or less forgot the incident until, weeks later, going in to see a chap named Blackburn, who was secretary to Thomas L. Kimball, then general passenger agent of the Union Pacific Railroad in Omaha, I was shown a scrapbook that Kimball kept, and in it was a clipping from the David City paper, quoting a part of my talk.

Not long thereafter Casper E. Yost, later an important figure in the American Telephone and Telegraph Company, told me that Senator Phineas W. Hitchcock wanted to see me. P. W. Hitchcock was Republican senator from Nebraska, and the father of Senator Gilbert M. Hitchcock, who was chairman of the Senate Committee on Foreign Affairs during the World War.

I found Hitchcock in the editorial rooms of the Omaha *Republican*, the paper in which he owned an interest, and he asked me to sit down. He leaned back in his chair and put the fingers of his hands together.

"Kyner," he began, "how would you like to go to the legislature?"

The question surprised me, but it appealed to me as well.

"Why, fine," I replied, "but I can't afford it."

For a time we talked, and he finally convinced me that I could. The pay was small, but such an office would take very little of my time. I agreed therefore, and within two years of my arrival in Omaha I was nominated at the convention. I was elected that fall with more votes, I remember, than were cast for the electors who elected Garfield president.

I took my seat in 1881, which was a period of great railroad activity, and legislation adverse to the railroads was forever being proposed. During my four years in the legislature I opposed all this, with more than a little success. Not one adverse act was passed while I was there.

In those days the Commercial Hotel in Lincoln was the rallying point of everyone in the legislature, and to the Commercial I consequently went. I asked for a room, but was told the place was filled. There were other hotels, of course, but the Commercial was *the* hotel, and so I wondered how I could manage to stay there.

John M. Thurston, later United States Senator from Nebraska, was, in 1881, the "political attorney" for the Union Pacific Railroad and was, as a matter of course, at the Commercial Hotel throughout the session. He was there, of course, to lobby for the railroad, and no better man could have been chosen. He had his own room and another beside it where he had such gatherings as he felt it necessary to call, and when I told him of my inability to get a room, he told me to use that meeting room of his, which I did, being sure to keep out of it when he required its use. The room, of course, was widely known, and someone named it the Union Pacific "oil room," a name that clung to it throughout the session.

There was in Lincoln then a man who formerly had lived in Omaha, where I had known him. Now, however, he was interested in local Lincoln politics, and was, as a matter of course, much about the Statehouse.

One day, meeting me in the corridor, he stopped me and, leading me off to one side, began to talk to me about the "Capitol Appropriation Bill" that was due to come up—a bill in which the Lancaster County delegation was interested. Lincoln, the state capital, lies in Lancaster County, and the local delegation forever had some bill up that would require the state to appropriate funds for local expenditure. This time it was for a new wing to the capitol, an addition that was about as necessary as two tails for a brindle pup.

My acquaintance talked to me about it for awhile, and finally said that the Lancaster County delegation had authorized him to make it worth my while to support the measure.

"Hm," I replied. "How much will it be worth?"

"I'll see that you get two hundred and fifty dollars," he replied.

I pretended to be doubtful.

"I'll have to think it over," I explained. "And this isn't any place to talk about it anyway. I'll tell you. You meet me in the Supreme Court room tomorrow at ten-thirty."

He agreed, and I, with a plan in my head, hurried off to see Bill Paxton, who also was a member of the House.

The Supreme Court was not in session, but in the courtroom, just to the right of the door, was a giant water cooler, where we often went to get a drink. I told Bill Paxton what had happened, and that I was to meet my man there the next day.

"Now I want you," I explained, "to be in there getting a drink, and I'll try to arrange it so that you can hear what we say."

Paxton agreed, and when, with my would-be briber, I entered the courtroom the next morning, Paxton, hardly obvious in the partly shadowed corner, was engaged in getting a drink. Strangely enough, our plan worked perfectly, and finally, when I felt that enough had been said, I stopped the conversation.

"No," I said. "No, no. I can't do it. I really can't."

I made certain, half an hour later, that Paxton had heard it all, and for the time being did nothing about it.

There was going on at this time an investigation of two members of the House from the western part of the state. The name of one of the men I have forgotten, but the other one was Robertson. Their constituents were very much opposed to some legislation favorable to the railroads, and had demanded that their representatives vote against the bill. When the bill had come up for a vote, however, Robertson and the other member did not appear and were reported "sick." Someone, suspicious of that "sickness," had gone to the hotel and, climbing on a chair in the hall, had looked through the transom into Robertson's room, to find him and the other ailing person thoroughly enjoying a beefsteak dinner.

"Beefsteak" Robertson he became from that time forth, and the investigation had to do with that pretended illness and the reasons therefor. He was telling a very plausible story about the matter, but unfortunately was unable to get any competent witnesses to swear that what he said was true.

The investigation was in full swing when, one evening in the crowded lobby of the Commercial, a member of the Lancaster County delegation named Searle saw me enter. He was a large man who spoke with a very loud voice, rather high in key, and it was with his voice somewhat louder even than usual that he addressed me on a subject for which I had long since prepared myself.

"Kyner," he bawled, his high voice reaching every corner of the lobby about which, in ten seconds, not another person was making a sound, "when we get through investigating Robertson we're going to investigate you and the Union Pacific 'oil room.' "

I had long been expecting something of the sort, and it did not take me by surprise as he may have expected it to do.

"Searle," I bawled out, imitating as best I could both the volume and the key of his voice, "I'll be glad to have you do that, and while you're investigating me and the Union Pacific 'oil room,' I'll rise to a question of privilege in the House and I'll say that a certain man—and I'll name him—came to me in the Supreme Court room and said he was authorized by the Lancaster County delegation to offer me two hundred and fifty dollars if I would support the 'Capitol Appropriation.' And then I'll call upon William A. Paxton and he will swear that what I say is true."

For a moment the crowded lobby was almost painfully quiet, and then the lid blew off. There were cheers and hurrahs and a buzz of loud talking. A dozen fellows slapped me on the back, and Searle, so far as I recall, did not answer a word, his breath knocked from him by his surprise.

Having gone that far, I was for pushing the matter further, and told Bill Paxton so. But he objected.

"No, no," he insisted. "No, no. Don't you do it. We've got 'em where we want 'em. That Lancaster crowd's been fightin' Omaha and Douglas County about everything. Just sit tight and make 'em toe the mark. They'll do it. They have to."

And they did. Through all the rest of that session, each time a bill came up that we favored or opposed all I had to do was to give the simplest sort of a nod or signal to Searle, and his crowd voted as a unit the way we did. I venture to say that there has never been another session of the Nebraska Legislature in which the Lancaster County delegation has shown so much thoughtful interest for the welfare of Douglas County and the state's major city.

Incidentally the man who had approached me had his career as a fixer brought abruptly to an end within an hour of that incident in the lobby of the Commercial Hotel.

Prohibition had not at this time reached the point to

which it later forced itself, and yet there were strong minorities who favored antiliquor legislation. At this session of the Nebraska Legislature a local option bill was up, and I opposed it, making a speech against it on a day when the galleries were well filled by earnest supporters of the measure.

I said what I thought, and was interrupted by a series of hisses from the galleries. It made me angry and I turned on them.

"Geese hiss!" I roared. "Snakes hiss, and so do fools! You in the galleries are occuping those seats as guests of this House. Remember, then, that you *are* guests, and do not attempt again either to intimidate or to encourage the members of this body. Should you do so I shall call upon the speaker to clear the galleries."

There were no more interruptions from the gallery—nor was there a sound, even when the bill passed. But I did not hear the last of it for some time. Someone was forever laughing at me and crying out "*Geese* hiss!"

Senator Hitchcock (the elder, of course,) was a man of wealth, and became interested about this time in obtaining the contract to construct all, or a major portion, of the Oregon Short Line. He spoke to me about it and wanted me to become his partner. It was an opportunity too good to be missed, and I was looking forward to it when he died quite suddenly.

His death left me somewhat at sea. His interest in railroad building, however, had aroused in me a desire to try my hand in that field—a field which, in those days, was one of enormous possibilities. Through Thomas L. Kimball, therefore, who had clipped the item from the David City paper, and who now was representing an important group of the owners of the Union Pacific

Railroad, I ultimately obtained a contract to construct twenty-five miles of branch line in Nebraska. I had no money with which to purchase my equipment. I had no experience whatever in railroad building. But with the friendly help of Bill Paxton, one of the wealthiest men in the state, I bought my equipment on credit, I bought my supplies on credit, and set out for the valley of the Loup River in central Nebraska to build twenty-five miles of railroad north and west from the little village of St. Paul.

6

IT WAS in June, 1881, that I went to work on my first railroad-building contract. I had obtained it, of course, because I had stopped some antirailroad legislation at Lincoln, and everyone knew that. The same sort of thing is being done in these days, but is glossed over and covered up by every sort of artifice. The older method, it seems to me, was better. I had nothing to hide, and made no effort to hide it. I believed that the railroads were vital to the development of the country, and my constituents knew I believed it. They knew, too, that I was now a railroad contractor. I have no doubt that having become a contractor may have made me a little more favorable to the railroads even than I had been—more partisan, perhaps, in their favor. But if that was true the difference it made in my beliefs was small, and certainly it was aboveboard.

Having shown my contract to William A. Paxton, I was told that it was a good one.

"Jim," he said, "that's a good contract. You ought to make some money."

It was on the strength of that contract that he had Paxton & Gallagher, the wholesale grocery establishment of which he was the chief owner, ship me on credit all the supplies I needed. He introduced me to other firms and had me refer still others to him. When I went to work at the little town of St. Paul, therefore, twenty or twenty-five miles from Grand Island which is on the main line of the Union Pacific, it was with a lot of supplies of all kinds for which I was in debt—supplies that I would have had some difficulty in gathering together without Bill Paxton's help.

I suppose every contractor has to begin sometime, but few have ever made a start with less information on the subject than I. I remember the first stake I looked at, there a hundred yards or so from the little depot at St. Paul. The stake stood just beyond the "railhead," and when I arrived I went over to take a look at it, in order to see what I was to do right there. A letter, some dots, and two numerals were printed on it: *C.1.5*. I stood there for a minute or more trying to interpret those hieroglyphics, but I could not. Had they been Latin or Greek I might have been able to recall enough of what I had been taught at college to make them out, but as it was I was utterly at sea.

I had other things to bother me, however, and for the time being put that problem aside, coming back to it now and then and wondering how I could get its message interpreted without giving my own inexperience and ignorance away.

Great piles of canned goods, flour, potatoes, tobacco, overalls, shirts, underwear, soap, and other things had been sent to me at St. Paul as a result of the orders I had left at Paxton & Gallagher and elsewhere. There was no freight bill, of course, for I was doing railroad work. Twenty drag scrapers had come, too, together with six wheel scrapers, two big steel railroad plows, and dozens of picks, shovels, and mattocks.

I needed help, of course, to check the invoices and to get the stuff in order, and going over to the little lumberyard that was one of the six or eight business enterprises of St. Paul, I hired a fellow named Jonathan Crowe to take charge of my commissary. It was a lucky move, for during all my twenty succeeding years as a contractor he kept that job. His wife, too, ran a local boardinghouse, and she was hired, consequently, to take over the feeding of my men, a task she retained as long as her husband worked for me.

The only workmen I could obtain were local men—farmers for the most part. I hired six or eight with teams at three dollars a day for man and team, and paid the other men a dollar and a half a day. There was not an old "terrier," as the professional railroad workers were called, until later when, hearing of the work that was going on off there on that branch line, they began to drift in. One man, however—Petersen by name—came in almost as soon as I arrived and asked for work. He was a small contractor himself, and had just finished building a little dam not far away. Furthermore, he had had a little railroad experience, so I hired him and the two teams he had, and at the first opportunity, pretending to be busy, sent him off to read that first stake with the *C.1.5.* on it, in the hope that his report might give me something that would make it possible for me, from then on, to read the others.

Whatever I was doing at the time was merely pretense, of course, and I remember how I watched him out of the corner of my eye. He strode off to the stake, glanced at it, and came back, while still I busied myself about my pretended task.

"Cut one and a half feet," he said, and I nodded solemnly, keeping my face as expressionless as I could in order not to show him how relieved I was.

The work was simple enough, but even simple work like that requires constant care to see that the men don't waste their time. I was being paid fourteen cents a yard for all the cuts and fills, hauling the dirt one hundred feet free, and receiving two cents per yard for every additional hundred feet of haul. With the single exception of Petersen, all the ninety or one hundred men I had were farmers, to whom efficiency was a thing unknown.

An efficiency expert was, of course, an unknown breed in 1881, and I had no name for what I was doing when I forced the men to make the shortest turns with their loaded scrapers, shouted at them to turn about the instant their scrapers had been dumped, saw to it that each scraper was loaded to capacity and that each load was hauled the shortest possible distance consistent with getting the work done.

I remember trying to get enough left-handed men to shovel into the wagons equally well from left or right. That problem bothered me until one of those natural handy men appeared upon the job. It made no difference to him which side he shoveled on, and I watched him for a time and saw him shift his hold from right to left and back again, depending upon which way he found himself working beside a wagon.

Right there I decided that all those shovelers would learn to do as that one man was doing, and before long they did. One or two of them got their time because they couldn't manage it, but within a week all the others had learned the trick.

The work we were doing was simple enough. There was no stone, no gravel—only the simple undulations of the sandy loam along the North Loup River—but it was surprising how hard it was to get enough small coin from the bank to pay the men. The first time I cashed a check at the local bank where I had set up an account, the man who ran it—Love by name—only with the greatest difficulty managed to get together the several thousands of dollars in silver that I required. I decided then and there to correct that, and on my next visit to Omaha cashed my check there and got it all in small bills and silver. I must have had two thousand or twenty-five hundred dollars in silver dollars, halves, and quarters.

It was a load, I can assure you—a load so great that I could not carry it by the handle of the valise—but by putting on a strap that I swung over my shoulder I got it to the train where I set it down in the aisle beside my seat, there being too little room under my feet, and the valise being too heavy for the rack above my head.

The big valise was in the way a bit, I do not doubt, and the brakeman coming through swung his hand down to lift it to the rack. He was perhaps a little off his balance when he took the handle. At any rate one pull sent him sprawling at full length in the aisle.

"Good Lord," he cried. "Have you got that nailed down?"

I told him that it was largely filled with silver dollars, and he had to admit that the danger of anyone's running off with it was slight. Never again, incidentally, did I have to go to Omaha for change. Those silver dollars and the smaller coins kept coming back to the bank in St. Paul in sufficient numbers to last through the eleven months that I was on the job.

I had, of course, a commissary from which my men could get supplies. Overalls, shirts, shoes, caps, tobacco, candy, canned goods—everything—and they were permitted to purchase anything they wanted and to charge it against their pay. It was a nuisance, however, and a time-consuming task for John Crowe to run and set down in his books every ten-cent purchase of tobacco and all the other trifling purchases they made. In order to save John's time I hit upon the scheme of printing scrip of my own, and in order to keep that scrip from being counterfeited, I had a new picture taken of myself, and had the picture printed on the back. These were printed in denominations of five, ten, fifteen, and twenty-five cents. Now Crowe, instead of setting down each little item, gave a dollar's worth or more of scrip to each man who used the commissary, charged that against him, and thereafter took the scrip as payment for the goods. It saved Crowe a lot of bookkeeping and was entirely satisfactory to the men. They seemed, in fact, heartily to approve of it, and used that scrip from then on in place of poker chips. How much "money" with my picture on it changed hands over the card tables during the following months I never knew, but it must have been a lot, for they were always playing. And too, they lost that scrip with far less worry than they lost real money—a thing not to be desired, I know, but something concerning which I did not trouble myself. Incidentally, a lot of it was never cashed.

I had, among the men working for me, a farmer boy named Josh Gray, as worthless a cuss as has ever been on my payroll. I thought many times of paying him off, but the loppy, easy-going, jolly lunkhead was so likeable, and so popular among the men—so willing, even if he was so inefficient—that I could not bring myself to do it. He would loll around the work until I shouted at him, and then, until my back was turned, he'd work like one possessed. But the moment I had left he would fall back into his easy-going ways and move a minimum of dirt. He lived with his mother, a gaunt, flat-breasted woman, in a little house a few miles off along the road I took to drive to St. Paul after we had worked away from town.

One day as I was driving past the place I saw her standing beside the road, and stopped when she called to me.

"Ain't you th' man that's a-buildin' this yere railroad?" she asked.

I admitted that I was.

"You know a feller up there named Josh Gray?" she went on.

I nodded.

"Well, he's my boy," she explained. "You tell him that th' old sow's been gittin' out of the pen and a takin' her pigs, and I'm a-gittin' tired a-chasin' 'round after her through the cornfield. You tell him I want him t' come right home and tend t' things, and t' leave that 'tarnal old railroad be right where it is."

I delivered the message, and Josh departed, but somehow, even without him, the work managed to continue.

We worked from June until winter was upon us, and by that time had graded about ten miles—out to a point where a chalk deposit lay beside the river. The survey called for a "side cut" through the chalk; that is, a cut along the steep slope and a fill on the side toward the North Loup River. Some limestone there gave us the stone we needed for the first riprap I ever had to construct, and the work in the chalk was not hard. We blasted it perfectly with dynamite, black powder blowing it out in pieces too big to handle, and as we cut along that bank we found several beaver houses, as clean and comfortable as anything I ever saw, built in the chalk itself.

The trappers of an earlier day had, of course, long since eliminated the beaver that once had lived along the North Loup River, but there the houses in that chalk formation were. The many floods that had passed since the beaver had been there had apparently cleared every sign of the former occupants away—every sign, that is, but the tooth marks in the chalk. The houses were three feet or so in diameter—eighteen inches or two feet high—and all of them communicated with the river by a little tunnel that ran down and came out below the water level. It suggested to me that beavers may be creatures of instinct to a lesser degree than might ordinarily be imagined.

By Christmastime we were working through that chalk, and my wife, wishing to spend Christmas with me, came out to St. Paul, leaving our two boys in Omaha with their grandmother. I worked hard all day Christmas, I remember, helping to build a wooden commissary shack at a spot to which the camp was to be moved. John Crowe, with his wife and children, was comfortably housed in a big sod house that stood near by. The men had, for the most part, left for the day, for all but a few lived on farms in the North Loup Valley.

Late in the afternoon I drove to town behind a horse I had bought not long before from the local livery stable keeper, and found my wife somewhat forlornly waiting for me at the bare hotel. St. Paul was, of course, not the most exciting place in the world. The village was the county seat of Howard County, but despite that it was very, very small; it had a bank, two or three stores, and a lumberyard. The hotel was a simple, two-story, frame affair, and in addition there were two agricultural implement shops, a harness shop, a livery stable—oh yes, and a doctor who, when I once went to him with an aching tooth, pulled the tooth next to it, much to my disgust.

But now I found my wife, somewhat lonely to be sure, in the very simple room I had in that very simple little hotel.

What a place to spend a Christmas! The town was as quiet as a tomb. In the hotel were only the proprietor and his wife; two poor devils of traveling salesmen, far from jovial because of being forced to spend the day away from home; the doctor, for whom that error with the tooth had aroused no admiration in my bosom; the keeper of the livery stable, who was not a bad sort; and the only Jewish saloonkeeper I ever saw. The latter was a flashy sport of the kind now long extinct, a follower of the horses, though there were few to follow in St. Paul, and a fancy dresser very obvious among the rest.

The wife of the proprietor, being a woman of some refinement, sensed the fact that my wife would not feel any too comfortable at table with that gathering, and though I had always been accustomed to eating my meals at the common board, we found, when we came down to supper, that a smaller table had been prepared for my wife and me.

Some attempt had been made at Christmas decorations, though holly, mistletoe, and all the rest were unobtainable in such a prairie village. I remember that some flowers were on our table, though where they could have come from I haven't the slightest idea.

Still, we were young—I only thirty-six and my wife thirty—and where, six years before, I had left Nebraska penniless save for the forty-eight dollars I received each six months from the government, now I was a person of some consequence: a member of the legislature, a railroad contractor; and where a dollar, six years before, had looked as big to me as the hind wheel on Father's biggest wagon, now I was the boss of a gang that required a payroll of more than three thousand dollars a month, and was making money with every flip of my shiny scrapers and every shovelful of dirt those men of mine were loading. Both of us, I know, had had worse Christmases, even though we wished we could be with our boys at home.

Cold weather forced us to suspend our work now and then. I tried to keep going, but the inspectors refused to measure fills made of frozen earth, which settle tremendously when warm weather comes. I struggled on, despite the fact that the railroad didn't pay me, and Love, the owner of that local bank, let me overdraw my account by three thousand dollars while I kept going. By plowing the "borrow pits" late every afternoon we could keep up with the grading, but still the inspectors would not report how much was done. Finally, on that account, I had to stop, but we were at it again at the first opportunity, and in May, 1882, the job was finished.

How well I remember finishing up the final duties of that task—paying bills, storing my equipment, paying off my men, closing the books. I went to the Union Pacific headquarters in Omaha for the final accounting, and going to the bank with my check I was asked how I wanted it.

"I'd like to have it," I said, "in a certificate of deposit made out to Naomi Kyner."

And that's the way I received it. I had graded twenty-five miles of railroad right of way in eleven months. I had bought and paid for all my many supplies and my equipment. I had paid some bills that I had owed before that contract started. And when I went home that afternoon in May, I dropped that certificate of deposit in my wife's lap.

She picked it up and read it. It was for $10,644.00.

She cried, I remember, for there was such a sum as we had never had before.

It would I think be somewhat surprising if, at this stage of the game, I had not thought rather well of myself, especially as, just as I was completing that twenty-five-mile contract, I was told of an opportunity to continue as a railroad contractor on the Oregon Short Line, which was then being built.

The Short Line was being financed, at least in a large part, by Sydney Dillon, the New York financier who had so great an interest in the Union Pacific. It was that connection between the Union Pacific and the Oregon Short Line that made me *persona grata* as a contractor.

I went out to Ogden, and from there to the end of track at American Falls. The bridge across the falls of the Snake River had been completed, but the track barely reached beyond it to a little camp of railroad engineers on the farther side. The road was surveyed and cross-sectioned by that time as far, I believe, as Boise, and I drove out for eighty miles across the desert looking over the land, preliminary to choosing some section of it to build.

Much of the way was, I knew, of a kind for which my limited experience had never fitted me—rock cuts and other work for which I had no equipment and concerning which I knew nothing. I chose, therefore, an eight-mile stretch which ended about five miles down Wood River from the town of Shoshone.

The question of supplies bothered me some, for the end of track was eighty miles away, and everything would have to be freighted across that waterless desert of lava rock and sagebrush, but when I asked about that in Omaha I was told that the track would be laid in another thirty days and that thereafter the question of supplies would be far simpler.

I shipped my equipment at once, therefore, even sending some of the men who had worked for me on the St. Paul job. I wasn't aware of the fact, but I had much to learn of railroad building, for it isn't every mile of track that is laid on easily graded sandy loam such as that above St. Paul in the North Loup Valley.

Instantly I ran into a hundred difficulties. The section I had chosen was, to the unaided eye, a simple task enough, but what difficult, unyielding stuff that lava rock turned out to be! Men, too, were hard to get, and what tough customers many of them were! No mild Nebraska farmers here, save the few I took with me. This was the gun-toting West, where heavy fists and six-shooters were the order of the day, and where the commonest drink was whiskey straight in large and potent quantities.

Rattlesnakes and horned toads, together with tarantulas and scorpions, helped not a bit to lighten the task, and thinking that the bite of any of these meant death, we were often uneasy because of them. One man—Force, by name—having been stung by a scorpion upon the calf of the leg—took out his knife and quickly carved something less than a pound of flesh from that part of his leg, but later we learned to fear these creatures less. Their stings are far from pleasant, but they usually left merely a white, hard spot the size of a silver dollar, and none of us died because of scorpions.

Early on that work I found that I couldn't handle those men the way I had handled my men in Nebraska. After the first payday the camp was literally filled with drunken men, full of fight. A fight in my former camp had been an almost unknown thing. Here they were constant—just after payday, anyway—and what brutal fights they were!

The work was horribly difficult as well, and a fool man with a twelve-mule team hitched to a brand-new plow that had cost me over a hundred dollars, swung the team to the side in the way he had often done to start a heavy wagon, only to break that plow before it had done a dollar's worth of work.

I was angry—worried, too, with the way the work was going—and as I got into my buckboard to drive back to camp from where the plow had been working, a tremendous "hammers man" who could swing an eight-pound hammer all day long, came up to me with some grievance of his own. I put him off and picked up the reins, but he swore at me.

"You're a ——— ——— coward," he roared.

He was standing near the buckboard, his great six-foot body a mass of muscle and sinew. I am not a small man, but he was larger and infinitely stronger than I. Still, no man could be permitted to talk to the boss like that, and I leaped. With all my weight behind the blow I struck him in the face. Down he went, but knowing that if he ever rose I was gone, I leaped astride of him, quite consciously bent on closing both his eyes before he could recover. I fairly well succeeded, too, before I was hauled off, and from that time I was boss, while pick-handle justice reigned.

The next payday more men were drunk, though I could not imagine where they got their liquor, away out there, miles and miles from anywhere. But finally I discovered that unknown to me a man had pitched a tent at the far end of camp, and that in it he had a considerable store of liquor.

Having learned of his being there I went to see him, told him how much trouble he was making, and asked him to move.

He refused and pointed to his license which he had tacked to his tent pole. It was a government license, and this was government land. Certainly, so far as legality was concerned, he was within his rights. Still, I tried to persuade him to move, and failing in that, asked him not to sell enough to get men drunk.

He still refused, insisting that he was there with his liquor and intended to sell it. I could see that there was no way to get rid of him except by force, and decided—legality or not—to *use* force.

I went back to where the dynamite was stored, got out a stick and cut it in two, picked up a fuse and a cap, and started back, boring a hole in the dynamite with my pencil as I went. I put the cap and fuse on, and lit a cigarette before I reached his tent.

I asked the fellow again if he would move, and was assured very positively that he would not.

"All right," I said. "If you won't move, I'll move you."

I fuzzed out the fuse, and still he said he wouldn't go. I lit the fuse from my cigarette, and held it.

"When this fuse gets down," I explained, "to the point where you won't dare pick it up, I'll toss her in."

"I'll move," he cried. "I'll move." And he began to scurry around.

The fuse by now was getting short and I tossed it off not far from his tent. It went off with a roar. The tent shook, and his horses, breaking loose, ran off a way.

"I'm going back to get another stick of dynamite," I shouted as he ran to get his horses. But I didn't need another. He packed up as quickly as he could, and disappeared, license and all.

The work throughout all that country was so hard and so costly that contractor after contractor was going broke. We were far from a bank, and were paying off with checks, but so many contractors' checks were bad that it was not long before the men objected to checks and demanded cash.

The difficulty brought about by this was greater than one might at first imagine, and I thought about the problem more than a little. The country was literally filled with bad men, and a payroll such as the one I had looked very attractive to such gentry. Robberies were common affairs, and I had no desire to have to carry cash in thousands of dollars across that desert. One could not hide the fact that the pay was due. Nor could one hide the fact that one was going to Ogden for it.

When I was next in Ogden, where the checks that were paid us were drawn on Guthrie, Dooly, and Company, I told Dooly of the problem, and asked him if I could get exchange on Boise. He assured me that I could. Guthrie, Dooly, and Company was an affiliate, somehow, of the Wells, Fargo Express Company. There was a similarly connected bank in Boise, and I could obtain exchange on them.

"How much will you charge me?" I asked.

"Three per cent," he told me, and preferring to pay the three per cent, even though the amount of my payroll was roughly five thousand dollars, to taking the risk incident to carrying it across the desert, I paid and got the draft.

I was somewhat relieved at having made the arrangement, for Boise was not so far from camp, and the money could be brought in from there with far less danger. But when I went to Boise to get it, the bank there charged me an additional five per cent, the two items together totaling more than four hundred dollars.

The amount was not enormous, it is true, but I was far behind on my work, losing money hand over fist, and it made me angry. My estimates were falling behind my payroll. I even had to go to Omaha to borrow some money, and on my way back, I stopped in Ogden, and seeing Dooly, told him in no uncertain terms what I thought of his exchange.

Perhaps I should not have done it, but at the time I know that I felt justified. However, I may have made it pretty strong. In fact, I know I did, and it made Dooly angry. I didn't care at the time, but I did later, for he got back at me in a way that I would have given another eight per cent or an even larger amount to have been able to avoid.

7

IT HAS often amused me in later years to see stage and motion-picture representations of the wild West of the days when I was building railroads. The uniformity with which gunmen of the screen wear chaps and swing their artillery in great holsters at their hips is laughable. But cowmen in chaps were always a very small minority in the West I knew, while gunmen more often carried their guns hidden than exposed. They were gunmen, however, for all of that, and some of them were as dangerous as even the movies make their villains out to be.

The nearest peace officer to the camp I had on Wood River was one hundred and twenty-five miles away, and it was up to the contractors in that day to be the law. We knew that bad men were about. John Crowe, who still kept books for me, used to tell me that each month when he opened the new time book many of the men who were working for me changed their names. Often they changed their jobs as well. From being teamster, perhaps, they would turn to shovel-and-pick work. We understood perfectly that these men were hiding from the law.

The country was filled with highwaymen, and every camp had men on the payroll who served as informers for these gangs of ruffians, in order that payrolls could be held up. So frequent and uniformly successful became the stagecoach holdups that the stages gave up the carrying of "treasure boxes," which made the task of bringing payrolls in even more uncertain. We all knew, from the frequent descriptions we heard, how such holdups were carried out. Five men—that seemed to be the usual number—all on horseback, would ride along the road to meet the coming victims. There was no hiding, usually, among the bowlders or the sagebrush. They merely jogged along in all innocence, apparently, toward the coming vehicle, and when it reached them, two men would rein out to one side of the road and three to the other. Then, as the stage started past, the driver suddenly found four rifles pointing at him. He would stop, of course, and the fifth man of the holdup gang, usually informed as to the valuables the stage carried, took the money. Payrolls were taken in the same way when they were being brought in by the contractors themselves, and I recall nothing that was ever done about it by "the law."

One particularly bad crime was committed not far from where I was working, and it illustrates the villainous depths to which such men could sink. The story came to me at second hand and I knew none of those affected, but it bears repeating for all of that.

A contractor working to the east of Shoshone, returning with his payroll, managed somehow to elude the gang that had set out after him, and reaching camp, where his wife and two little daughters were staying at the time, put the money safely out of sight. The highwaymen, however, followed him to camp, where the contractor had set up his family in tents at some distance from where the workmen were housed.

So surprising and brazen was this entry into camp that the family was taken off guard, but the money was hidden, and even with a gun under his nose the contractor refused to tell where it was. The highwaymen, consequently, decided to force him to reveal its hiding place, so they put a noose about his neck, ran two wagons together so that their tongues could be lashed in the form of a huge inverted V, and proceeded to pull the unlucky fellow up, thinking to give him a taste of the rope and thus to force the secret from him. Unluckily, however, the rope wedged tight somehow, and there the contractor was strangled to death before his wife and daughters, not one of whom, because of the guns held on them, had dared scream for help.

The highwaymen did not, I believe, get the money, but that by now had become a small matter. Still, not a thing was ever done about that brutal crime. A new contractor took over the work, and the matter was more or less forgotten, save, of course, by that unfortunate woman and those two poor girls.

With such things going on about me I was given food for thought. I had never carried a gun, and had no desire to carry one now, but I had to. I purchased a handsome, single-action .44, therefore, the very next time I went to Omaha, and began to practise—very privately—until I learned to use the weapon.

Quickness with a revolver being essential if it should be of service in a pinch, I practised pulling the trigger as I swung the gun down, and the amount of powder I burned in practice was enormous. From the commissary I obtained the circular pieces of cardboard that came between the layers of crackers in the cracker barrels, and hanging one of these on a sagebrush or greasewood branch, I'd pace off twenty or thirty steps and go to work.

It took me a long time to get the hang of it, but finally

it came, and ultimately I could hit those cardboard targets a good deal oftener than I missed them. Still, I had no desire to be a gunman, and thought that if the men about knew I could shoot, there would be less likelihood of my being called upon to do so seriously. I therefore continued my practice somewhat more openly—on Sundays or other times when the men were not at work. I would take my target off among the sagebrush as if in search of seclusion, but so I could be seen from camp. A few shots would attract attention, of course, and soon a man or two would drift my way. Others would follow, and others still, until a good-sized audience had collected, while I was doing my best to fill that cardboard full of holes. Fifteen or twenty holes in such a target make it look very impressive, I can assure you, and I began to impress the men. And then, finally, I got what I was really aiming at when I heard, for the first time, a man turn to his partner and say "By God, Bill, I wouldn't want the old man to be a-shootin' at me."

During all the time I was railroading in the West I never drank and never sat at a gambling table. Countless times, and of necessity, I visited saloons, for it was about the saloons that everyone congregated, and I was forever hunting for men to work for me.

On one occasion, needing some men after a payday, I took a teamster and a wagon with me into the town of Shoshone, and leaving the teamster to his own devices, I entered the Lava Rock Saloon.

This—quite the most "polite" of the town's saloons—was a one-story building built of the omnipresent lava rock, its black, cast-iron-colored walls enclosing a room that was roughly twenty by sixty feet in size. The proprietor, a very pleasant sort of chap, told me on one occasion that his wife and daughters lived in Illinois, but that they were decent folks whom he had never told about the saloon. He had told them, so he said, that he was running a mill, and so he was—a gin mill that was always a very well-patronized place. He himself, however, never took a drink, and none of the town's many "girls" were ever to be seen at the Lava Rock. "Pink's Place" and others housed that trade. There was, however, a rule in the Lava Rock that whenever a man invited the house to drink with him, everyone must comply or risk dancing to the tune of a revolver shooting at his feet.

On this occasion, however, I had no sooner entered the well-filled Lava Rock than I encountered Frank Luddington, a contractor who had taken a subcontract from me. Frank was a delightful fellow, a nephew of General Luddington who at that time was Quartermaster General of the U. S. Army. He asked me what I was doing in town, and I told him I was after men.

We were talking of the work we were doing and standing a few feet from the bar, behind which six bartenders were busily engaged, when one of those rare, chaps-wearing, gun-toting cowpunchers rolled up to the bar, and slapping a twenty-dollar gold piece down, waved his hat in the air.

"Everybody drinks with me!" he bawled. "Everybody drinks with me!"

There was a scuffling of feet and a scraping of chairs that told plainly that his all-inclusive invitation was being accepted, and the cowpuncher, pleased apparently at being the center of attraction, turned to me.

"Everybody drinks with me!" he bawled again. "Step up. Step up. What'll ye have?"

He was a young fellow who should have had better

sense, but he didn't and I had no intention of accepting his invitation.

"Oh no, son," I replied. "I don't want anything."

"Oh, you got t' have something," he insisted. "Got t' have something."

"All right," I replied. "Bartender, give me a box of matches."

The cowpuncher let out a whoop of delight.

"That's a good one," he yelled, and slapped me on the back. "That's a good one. But it's all right."

And he circulated uncertainly among his many guests.

"Great Caesar, Jim," grumbled Luddington, picking up his glass. "You've got your nerve. Don't you know the rule of this place?"

"Sure I know it," I replied. "But rules like that are not always as positive as they sound."

I was not at that time an "old-timer" in the West, and much of it was new to me. I was often told by others, however—men who knew the West from *A* to *izzard*—mining camps, cow camps, boom towns, and railroad camps—that Shoshone was in those days quite the toughest of the lot. Certainly if any other place was tougher it was very tough indeed. Stabbings and shootings were common occurrences. A cemetery among the sagebrush near by was well populated by men who had died with their boots on.

"Every man in it," I was told once, "has died a violent death except one fellow who got drunk, fell in the river, and was drowned."

Even that fatality did not impress me as the quietest of deaths.

There were said to be, during my time in the vicinity, about five thousand people in Shoshone, and it was a commonplace remark that there was not a respectable woman in the town. Yet rough and low as so many of those men and women were, they respected in others what they themselves had never had or had long since lost.

My wife, on one occasion, came from Omaha to visit me at camp, and one day we drove together to Shoshone. We arrived about noon, and having no food with us, I asked O. S. Lyman, a nephew of Sydney Dillon, whether or not he and his associates had a "mess" at which my wife and I could eat.

He seemed a bit perturbed.

"No," he replied. "We eat at a restaurant behind a saloon. The food is good enough, but it's hardly a place for your wife."

Still, no other solution to the problem being offered, we decided to try it, and Lyman led us to where a big tent housed the saloon he spoke of. We entered, walked past the bar and, pulling aside a fold of the canvas tent wall, entered a still larger tent filled with crowded tables at which sat scores of loudly talking men, with more than a scattering of women. Profanity and loud voices filled the air, but within five seconds of our entry almost every sound had ceased. Only a drunken fellow at a table with a girl let out another profane yip or two, and the girl, reaching over and shaking his shoulder, tipped her head in our direction. Whereupon even he fell silent.

A waiter led us to a table, and the place resumed a part of its former activity, but during the half-hour or so that we were there there was not another profane word or another objectionable remark.

Outside again, Lyman shook his head.

"For a long time," he remarked, "I've been ashamed of a lot of Americans I've seen here. But after what I've just seen I have more respect for the riffraff of this country than I ever had before."

"Pink's Place" was the most spectacular in Shoshone. It contained a bar, and in the same room were the "Wheel of Fortune" and the faro and stud poker tables. It was a two-story structure, and upstairs was the rookery occupied by the girls of the place.

The owner was one Pinkston, who was recognized throughout the country as the head of an organized band of considerable size—a band made up of gamblers and highwaymen who laid the whole region under tribute. It seems strange to me—and did at the time—that such conditions could exist when agents of the Department of Justice and the Department of the Interior were always to be seen in Shoshone, while "secret service" representatives of the Union Pacific were there as well.

Pinkston himself was not a large man. He was clean, trim, active, and was, I think, the handsomest man I ever saw. I remember talking to him only twice—both times when I had entered his place in search of men. But from those two conversations it seemed obvious to me that he was both well-bred and well-educated. He was smooth-shaven, with very dark hair and the fairest sort of skin, and his face, instead of growing red when he drank, grew as white as that of a woman. His clothes were tailor-made, and were always quiet, and I distinctly recall that while the custom among men was to wear enormously heavy gold watch chains, his was slender and unobtrusive. His manner, too, was quiet, and he talked little. His gun, if he wore one—and I have no doubt he did—was never in evidence.

On a third occasion, going there for men, I met the person known as "Pink's woman." Whether she was his wife or not I do not know, but in some ways she was like him. Among the painted creatures that filled the place she stood apart—soft-spoken, rather pretty, pleasantly dressed. When I asked for Pinkston she told me he was busy and nodded to where he sat in a game of cards. She then asked if she could do anything for me, and when I told her I needed men, she rounded some up for me, and did it very quietly and efficiently.

But despite the apparent gentility of these two, "Pink's Place" was headquarters for the criminals of the region. It had been built before the railroad reached the town, and the coming of the railroad seemed but to add to its opportunities.

With the opening of the depot, a man named Nichols had become agent—a man so perfectly fitted for such a task that he seemed invariably to be chosen by the railroad for that task at whatever town happened to be at the railhead, for there, usually, the most difficult problems for a station agent had to be faced, and the roughest element had to be handled.

Nichols, some years before, with a man named Valentine, who now was in Shoshone in the secret service of the Union Pacific, had captured nine of the ten men who made up the villainous Olive gang who had operated about Plum Creek (now Lexington), Nebraska. Val had been a hotel clerk there, and Nick had been station agent, when the state, aroused at the brutal hanging and burning of a man by Ike Olive and his cohorts, had set a reward of ten thousand dollars on their heads.

Nichols and Valentine, getting their heads together, decided to get those men, and when Ike Olive, coming into the hotel, was told by Val to put his hands up, he was slow about it, not knowing that a signal from Val had called Nick from the near-by station. The bad man, as Nichols told me later, was apparently considering some method of attack or retreat when Nick, with a Winchester rifle, slipped noiselessly up behind him.

"Put 'em up, Isaac. Put 'em up," Nick ordered, holding his rifle within a foot of Olive's back. "I'm a-gettin' nervous and this damn' thing may go off."

Turning to find that second gun upon him, Olive surrendered, and between them the two ultimately captured nine of the ten men. But never a cent of the ten thousand dollars did they get, the penurious authorities in Nebraska insisting that the reward was for *all ten*.

I was accidentally almost within arm's length of the final outcome of this affair, which took place at Blackfoot, near Fort Hall, and not many miles from Shoshone.

Going there one day on some business or other I met Valentine, and asking him what he was doing there, I got a typical reply.

"Just lookin' 'round," he said. But finally he told me more.

"Last night," he said, "I walked over to that saloon—" he pointed across the track "—and when I went in I saw some fellows playin' cards. I got a cigar and was leanin' against the bar talkin' to the bartender, when one of those fellows got up and came to the bar, too. He ordered a drink, and talking to the bartender, he said: 'I've seen men with whiskers all over their faces, and I've seen 'em with their faces shaved smooth. But, by God, I always know 'em.' He tossed off his drink and went back to his table, and I began to wonder how I could get out of there without turnin' my back on him."

"Who was it?" I asked.

"The only man we didn't get in Ike Olive's gang," he replied.

"What did you do?"

"Well, after awhile I walked out as if I hadn't heard a word, but I took a long breath when I got across the track. And then I went to the hotel and wrote him a note that I sent over to the bartender by a boy."

"What did you say?"

Val almost smiled.

"I told him," he said slowly, "that I was workin' for the U. P. and not for Nebraska any more. And then I said I'd known for two years where he was, but that he was perfectly safe as far as I was concerned."

It was this man and Nichols, the station agent, who had the responsibility of looking out for the railroad's interest in and about Shoshone, and two better men for the task could hardly have been found. Nick, a clever hand at the telegraph key, was just as clever with his gun—and needed to be.

After the road had been opened as far as Shoshone I did not visit the town for some time, but going in, finally, I dropped in to see Nick at the station just before train time, and knowing him well, went into his office, with its ticket window and its big bay window where the telegraph instrument stood and from which the agent, even when he was at his key, could see plainly both up and down the track. Pink's gang had been pretty active of late, I knew, though I was soon to learn more.

We talked for a few minutes and finally Nick glanced up at the clock.

"The train's about due," he said, "and I guess you'd better go over across the track to those stores."

"Why?" I asked, in some surprise.

"Well, Pink's gang has been holdin' up the passengers when they get off," he explained, "and I've got orders from the company to clear the platform when the train comes in."

It was the first that I had heard of passengers being held up quite so publicly, and I suspect that it had happened only once. I suspect, too, that Nick had wired the suggestion that he be ordered to clear the platform. Still, it looked like a big order to me, and I said so.

"I'll stay and help you," I offered.

"No, no," he objected. "You go across the track. I don't want anybody gettin' in my way."

I suggested that he let me stay in the office.

"All right," he agreed. "But don't you come out."

I agreed, and as he left, I sat on the corner of the telegraph table and watched through the window.

Nick, as did many of the men most feared by the lawless element, wore a double-breasted coat, in each side pocket of which he carried a gun. What guns he carried, I do not know. Derringers, being hammerless, were often used that way, and he may have had them. But whether he did or not I saw him, as he stepped upon the platform, with his coat buttoned and with his hands in his side pockets.

The train was already in sight down the track and a dozen or fourteen men were on the platform. It was, perhaps, significant that many more people were in front of the stores beyond the track.

I watched intently, keyed up myself at the task Nick was so coolly tackling, and saw him walk steadily toward the group of men.

"I've got orders," he said, in a voice that sounded as

cold and hard as steel, "to clear the platform when the train comes in, so you fellows get off here, and do it now!"

The group was obviously surprised, and for a moment they hesitated as Nick continued to advance. Then they backed off, and when a few seconds later the train pulled in, Nick was alone on the long platform.

I have told all this in order to show that building railroads in Idaho in the eighties presented other problems than merely those imposed by lava rock and lack of water. But the physical difficulties were in themselves enormous. I was told later that the building of the Oregon Short Line cost three million dollars more than the construction company paid for it, and I believe it. I know that I contributed my share on that first contract I had—more than my share, I thought at the time. Though it didn't quite break me, it broke many others.

The contract I had taken made it possible for us to get water easily, for we were working along Wood River, but some of the contractors working out on the desert had one team hauling water for each team they had on the dump, and the supplies for all of us had to be wagon-freighted for months and months longer than I had been told they would. I had been told, when I started, that the track would be laid in thirty days, but six months later a reorganization of the track-laying work had to be made in order to get results.

I had, as I have said, chosen the section on which I was working, because the work appeared light, but the moment we started, that lava rock taught us something. Furthermore, it was necessary to do more than cut through that. A railroad track laid directly on such unyielding stuff would ruin the rolling stock in no time.

No locomotive could stand the punishment. We were forced, therefore, to go a foot or so below grade, and then fill in with earth. And how we scratched about to get the necessary material to make up that foot! I learned then how meagre is the supply of sand and soil over that awful lava rock.

The rock itself necessitated the use of enormously high explosive powders. Black powder did little but heave up blocks too big to handle. It had to be shattered by a sharper explosion, and even then the stuff seemed keyed together until it was almost impossible to load it and haul it away.

Time after time my payroll fell behind the estimates, and finally I had to go to Omaha to borrow some money in order to continue. I managed to get it, and on my way back, my wife went with me. It was then, when we reached Ogden, that I drew from Guthrie, Dooly, and Company what little still remained there to my credit and read the riot act to Dooly about his exchange on Boise. Then, going over to Kelton, Utah, on the Central Pacific—the Southern Pacific now (this was, of course, before the Oregon Short Line had been opened to Shoshone)—we took the stage for Starrs Ferry on the Snake River where I had arranged to be met by my own team and buckboard.

My wife and I had quite a sum with us—some thousands of dollars—and naturally wondered how it could best be guarded. Ultimately we divided it, and while she pinned some to some inner garment and carried it thus across her back, I rolled up all I could and thrust it down into the cavity of my artificial leg.

We got the stage in the early afternoon and in that lurching, swaying thing we rode across the Goose Creek

Range without a stop, except to change horses, until breakfast time next morning when we arrived at Starrs Ferry. Then after a very short stop, we got into my buckboard—one I had had made to order for the hard going of that almost roadless country—and started out to drive across the desert before dark.

I had an excellent team, and off across that treeless, waterless, deserted land we drove. I held the reins, and how I drove those willing animals! Later they covered many more miles in a day for me—very many more, but it was not across such country as that Idaho desert.

We reached camp at dusk that evening, my wife so worn and tired as almost to be ill, and I was more than willing to get to bed myself. The horses, I remember, were no sooner unhitched, watered, and turned loose than both of them headed straight for Wood River and plunged in.

The physical strain of sixteen hours in the rattling, swaying, jerking coach, with eight more in that bouncing, careening buckboard would in itself have been enough to tire us out, but the strain of carrying that money through such a land was worse. If that had been lost, I was liable to be lost as well, and I realized it most thoroughly.

The difficulties of the work continued, and if anything, became more exasperating. Blasts sometimes barely cracked the surface of the rock, blowing down, instead, into openings—ancient bubbles, perhaps—in the lava itself. Men were harder than ever to get, and after every payday the shortage of men was always troublesome. The railroad shipped hundreds of men from the East, many with their horses and wagons, but when they reached the railhead many of those fellows never stopped to work at all, but drove on to Oregon and Washington, having had their railroad transportation free to the end of the track.

Wagon freighting was always a problem, with not nearly enough freighters to carry the enormous quantities of supplies required by the contractors. Baled hay that had been obtained for six dollars a ton in Nebraska cost me a hundred dollars a ton by the time it was piled in my camp. For every dollar that I spent in the purchase of case goods, more than two dollars was spent in getting it to camp.

On one occasion, having ordered a carload of powder, I particularly inspected it when it had arrived, and found that the jarring, jolting wagons had worn holes through the sheet-steel kegs so that more than two inches of powder had sifted out into the bottom of the wagon box. In that same wagon, to my amazement, I found a half-used candle stuck in its own wax to a powder keg. By the light of that candle, when he had stopped for the night, the driver had read for a time before going to sleep upon the powder kegs which contained enough explosive to have blown him well up toward the Milky Way.

The freighting done by the professional freighters was slow and costly business. A twelve-horse team, hauling a great wagon holding five thousand pounds, and trailing either one or two smaller wagons with lesser loads, made up a unit. The driver rode the "nigh wheeler" and guided all those animals at will by signals on the jerk line —a long rope leading forward to the "nigh leader." Merely by jerks on that line and by his voice he drove, while a "swamper," on the big wagon, set and released brakes, and performed the other tasks that so considerable an outfit demanded.

Often, however, despite the high rates we paid, such

freighters were not to be had at all, and then, with supplies imperatively required, I often had to take men off the work, send them to American Falls, and wait four or five days for their return.

It is no wonder that throughout the building of that eight-mile stretch I constantly lost money. With every setting of the sun my load of indebtedness was growing.

8

THE DETAILS of that work along Wood River became thoroughly embedded in my mind, for it was a struggle from the first—a struggle in which that $10,644.00 that I had dropped into my wife's lap disappeared like water on the desert, and was followed by debts and borrowed money until I began to wonder whether there was any way to make anything on the Oregon Short Line after all.

In the very midst of all this unprofitable work and all the worry that it entailed I had to have a fool experience that did not help much, either. It was during the winter of 1882-83, and I had gone into the commissary tent one day to look at the books. Stitt, the bookkeeper—John Crowe's job as keeper of the commissary had grown so big that he could attend to nothing else beside the men's time—had his desk at the end of the long counter that ran the length of one side of that big eighteen-by-thirty-foot tent. Behind the counter the shelves and boxes of supplies stood before the six-foot canvas wall. The big lamps that illuminated the tent during the long, cold evenings had not yet been lighted, and the big square stove that Stitt spent so much time filling with sagebrush and alder was doing its best to take some of the chill off the dry air.

Before the counter the tent was largely vacant, with plenty of space for the men when they came in to make their purchases, and several men were there, including a fellow whom I never knew except as John—a quiet sort of fellow, I had always thought, who worked for me as a scraper holder. He was dressed in overalls, I remember, and wore a dark woolen shirt, and having somehow got his hands on a cheap, nickel-plated revolver, was showing it off. He was talking about it and pointing it here and there with awkward flourishes in an attempt to show his ability with the weapon, and suddenly—though for what reason I had not the slightest idea—I found it pointing directly at me. It was within two feet of my face, and distinctly I could see the round dull balls in the loaded cylinder.

Now loaded revolvers—or unloaded ones either, for that matter—have no business pointing in men's faces, and I brought my hand down on it as quickly as I could. There was a report; I felt a burning blow in the thigh of my left leg—my good one—and down I went. Stitt and Crowe and some others rushed to where I lay and carried me presently to my tent, which stood near by.

The ball, which was a .32, or possibly even smaller, had passed through my thigh, though luckily without touching the bone, and for four or five days I was laid up, with the result that, being inactive, I could think about my problems to better advantage, though with no better results that I recall.

In their efforts to help me, no one had grabbed John, and when they went to look for him the fellow had lit out—without his pay—without even his few belongings.

The reason was not far to seek. He had had, the men all assured me, no intention of shooting me; but when the revolver had gone off and I had fallen, I had loosed a volley of profanity and had told him, in forceful Western terminology, that I would "get" him. Probably he had seen me practising on the cardboards from the cracker barrels and feared to remain. At any rate he never appeared again.

Mrs. Force, the wife of the subcontractor who had cut the section of flesh from his leg when the scorpion had stung him, attended to my wound, for there was no doctor about. What she did for it I don't know, but I was quite sound again within two weeks or so.

The end of the work along Wood River was within sight when I went to Omaha again to get some more money, and to check up on the bills I owed. It was downright disheartening. Every cent I had had was gone, and the loans at the bank, together with the bills I owed to Paxton and Gallagher and other firms, totaled sixty-three thousand dollars, a sum so vast to me—and to most others in the eighties—as to seem cast in astronomical figures.

I told Mr. Clark about it when I went to see him at Union Pacific headquarters, and I remember that he seemed somewhat perturbed. A large part—probably the major part—of that loss was due to the delay in the laying of the track, and he obviously felt somewhat responsible for the loss. He offered, at any rate, to send an auditor out to check my books in order to see what could be done, and I went home to tell my wife about it.

"Why Jim," she asked when I had told her, "what on earth will you do?"

"Well, 'Omi," I replied, "I don't know of but one way to get rid of a debt."

"What's that?" she asked.

"Pay it," I replied.

I remember that she shook her head, and tears were in her eyes.

"We'll be paying debts," she said somewhat mournfully, "as long as we live."

"Oh, no we won't," I insisted confidently. "Oh, no we won't."

But I had no clear idea, I'll have to admit, of what would prevent it.

I returned to Wood River, and Clark, true to his word, sent the auditor. My books were checked with the greatest care, and as a result I got a check for a little over nine thousand dollars—partial payment, at least, for that delay in track building. It still left me far in the hole, of course, but it helped some, and then, without my having asked for it or even knowing about it, they gave me a contract for thirty miles of construction far up the main line beyond Mountain Home, not very far from Boise.

A contract for thirty miles of railroad was tremendously big for me. As a matter of fact, it was far from small for any contractor, and when I went to look it over I almost danced with delight. It had been that awful lava rock along Wood River that had made the trouble—that lava rock and the bills for wagon freighting.

But now, the day I was finishing that eight-mile stretch, the rail-laying gang reached me, and stopped for one day just as they reached my work. I asked the man in charge—Jim Way by name, and a friendly and highly efficient fellow—why he was stopping.

"We're out of spikes," he told me, but to this day I believe he wasn't. He was not the sort who runs out of supplies. My belief is that he gave that reason in order to keep from charging that delay to me, for he knew, as well as everyone else, what a licking I had already taken. Years later I told him what I thought, and he pretended to grow angry at me for believing such a thing. Yet I still believe it.

But now I had the new contract, and what an opportunity it was. Thirty miles of work without enough rock in it for me to remember now. I doubt if there was any, but I can't be certain of that. Certainly there was little, and possibly there was none, and they paid me twenty-five cents a yard.

How we made that Idaho dirt fly! We ran into some hardpan we could not plow, I remember, and we "shot" it. But once a little powder had been used it went perfectly. I greatly enlarged my outfit, and during a long period of time had so many horses at work there that it took three tons of oats a day to feed them, and three tons of oats, you may be sure, make quite a pile in any farmer's bin.

Hay, by good fortune, we did not need, for among the sagebrush and greasewood the bunch grass grew, and by night-herding the horses, we took advantage of that. They worked all day and ate that bunch grass during most of the night, sleeping on their feet for the most part after four o'clock or so in the morning.

What hours we worked! Ten hours a day and six days every week with scrapers and wheel scrapers doing most of it.

What a relief it was to move from Wood River to Indian Creek! Where formerly we had struggled and worked and worried through that lava rock, with Hell on wheels not far away at Shoshone, now we had such work as railroad men might pray for, with Boise fifteen or eighteen miles away. And Boise, to those of us accustomed to the desert, was almost Paradise.

The town was situated in what was, in fact, a beautiful oasis, with fruit trees and beautiful green lawns in profusion. It was beautiful in its own right, but to those of us who visited it after living amid the dust and sagebrush of the desert it was unbelievable perfection. One street at the edge of town had a ditch of running water down its center, and along that ditch at intervals were little "King David" wheels, operated by the current and constantly dipping up the water and pouring it into little lateral waterways that ran beneath the road surface to the bright green lawns. Water ran in ditches along both sides of the main business street—a sight to delight us when we came in from the parched plains.

Neither was there any of that wild West hurrah that was so insistent a characteristic of Shoshone. What brawling, drunkenness, and lewdness there may have been in Boise was either hidden from the sight of decent folk or amounted to very little. All the railroad camps were liberally supplied with tough characters, of course, but Boise, at least, seemed remarkably free of them.

The town was supplied by wagon freighters, and Boise without the great wagons and twelve-horse teams would not have been the Boise I knew then. But the homes of frame and brick were comfortable and attractive, and the town stands out in my mind as quite the most attractive of any that I ever saw in all that vast expanse from the Missouri to the mountain ranges closest to the coast. The governor of Idaho at the time was Jack Neil, who had been, twenty-two years before, the adjutant of my regiment in the Civil War. I went to see him only once, but he was away on a hunt, and though I planned to go again, I never did.

The railroad was being pushed to completion as rapidly as possible, and all the pressure that could be brought to bear was directed at those of us who were doing the work north and west of Mountain Home. These last few miles would connect the Oregon Short Line with the Oregon Railroad and Navigation Company, the terminus of which lay not many miles beyond where I was working.

I had a number of subcontractors working for me, and had taken as a "partial partner" a man named Doty, when I learned to my surprise that another—and a very influential contractor—had moved onto a portion of that thirty miles assigned to me, and with his big outfit was making more progress than I was. I should, perhaps, have made a complaint, but I did not. The result was that I did a little less than half that work, but so profitable was it that I was doing very well, despite the loss of so many miles. The incident illustrates as clearly as anything the viewpoint all of us had in the Idaho of those days. When we knew what we wanted we merely went and got it, and that is what that other fellow did, and I, being both busy and quite successful on the portion that remained, did not disturb him.

There was, however, a difficulty arising of which we contractors knew nothing, and it was not until a month or so before I finished up that I learned enough to figure out the thing.

We were paid each month by a disbursing agent in Ogden—a clerk named Strome being the man who actually attended to the details. Strome had nothing to do with it but to keep the accounts and pay the amounts called for by our "estimates." The estimates were the reports made by the engineers of how much work we had actually completed, measured in cubic yards and in the distances we had to haul beyond the hundred yards that was required of us.

Going to Ogden a month or so before the job was completed, I was handed an estimate so greatly below what I knew I had done that I could not imagine what was wrong, and Doty, my partner, who was with me, almost had a fit. He was, I must admit, a nervous chap naturally, and when he saw that the amount the estimate said was due would not nearly pay the men, he had good reasons for his nervousness.

Many contractors, as I have said, had gone bankrupt on that line, and many a time the workmen had performed all sorts of cruelties when their money had not been forthcoming. And Doty had his family at camp—a family that he might never get away from there if we went back without our money. My wife and sons were safe in Omaha, and whatever arose I had only myself to guard, but Doty was less fortunate.

The estimate bothered me, you can be sure, and I spoke to Strome about it.

"This won't come anywhere near meeting our payroll," I insisted. "There *must* be something wrong."

He was noncommittal, and I sat down in the lobby outside the partition that cut the office in two, to study the matter a bit.

As I sat there another contractor came in—Ed Corrigan by name—and a member of the firm of Corrigan and Carlisle. Corrigan was a capable fellow, rough enough to stand out among the rough men in that country, and his partner, Carlisle, had formerly been governor of

Colorado. Altogether they were a pair that had no need to fear even the powers behind the Union Pacific and the Oregon Short Line, for they were well established—even wealthy.

Corrigan, wiser than I, had obtained a copy of the estimate on his work from the engineers who made the report—had accompanied them over the work and knew that it was right. He demanded his check, therefore, and when Strome hesitated, a hot and quarrelsome argument began. Obviously Strome did not want to make out so great a check, but Corrigan demanded it and finally obtained it.

That Strome was troubled was plain, but finally he made the check out, and handed it over.

"What are you going to do with it?" he asked as Corrigan took it.

"That's my business," replied Corrigan. "I'm going to cash it," he went on. "And if they won't pay it, they'll protest it."

I was listening quite frankly, and for the first time a little glimmer of light broke in upon my befuddled brain. As Corrigan left the office, therefore, which was on the second floor of a building next door to the bank of Guthrie, Dooly, and Company, on whom our checks were drawn, I got up and followed him, stopping on the sidewalk when Corrigan entered the bank.

I had not waited more than a minute or two when Dooly, hatless and in a hurry, came out the door and hurried up the stairs to Strome's office, and Corrigan, frowning and plainly angry, came out of the bank and stood waiting impatiently near me.

"Are you going to get your money?" I asked.

"Oh, they'll pay me," he growled, "or I'll put 'em in a hole."

And now, still perturbed and hurrying, Dooly reappeared. He went into the bank with Corrigan at his heels, and presently Corrigan reappeared as Carlisle, his partner, came across the street. The first remark that Corrigan made told me that he had obtained his money, and I turned about and thoughtfully climbed the stairs to Strome's office once more.

The conclusion I drew was reasonably obvious by now. Dillon, in New York, was having difficulty in getting the road financed, and now, with so little left to do, the treasury was empty. The estimates, therefore, were being cut down in order to make the contractors carry the load until the New York financiers could somehow raise more. Corrigan, however, with his big outfit and his wisdom in seeing that his estimate was accurate, had managed to obtain a check for an amount greater than was credited to the construction company, and Dooly, having at first refused to cash it, had been asked to protest it. This, however, he had not dared to do, for the news of that protested check would have flown across the country with the very breeze.

However, all that did not help me. I had not obtained my estimate as Corrigan had, and had no way of correcting it now. I went, therefore, to Strome's window again, and spoke to him.

"Strome," I said, "there's something wrong with my estimate, but I don't know how to get it fixed now. I've got to have some money. I don't dare to go back to camp without it. Where can I borrow some?"

I suspect he knew from Dooly that I was no longer

in the good graces of Guthrie, Dooly, and Company. At any rate he never mentioned them.

"Why don't you go over to Young's bank?" he asked, meaning the First National Bank of Ogden.

I nodded and went out, determined to try, though it seemed silly that a person no better known in Ogden than I was could walk into a bank he had never entered before, and get a loan from men he'd never seen, especially when the amount I wanted was eighteen thousand dollars. Nevertheless I went, and once inside I asked for Mr. Young.

He greeted me quietly and when I had told him who and what I was, asked me to be seated.

I thereupon, as simply as I could, told him that I wanted to borrow eighteen thousand dollars on my note.

He asked me who would sign it, and knowing no one else in Ogden, I told him I thought Strome would—Strome the clerk, who lived in a rented house and hadn't a thing in the world but his monthly pay check, which probably was none too large.

"Sorry," he said, though somehow I gathered that Strome as a signer was satisfactory, "but our bank limits such notes to ten thousand dollars."

That stumped me for a moment; but suddenly a wild, a preposterous, idea came to me.

"Well," I began. "Could you let me have ten thousand dollars on my note, with Strome to sign it, and advance eight thousand dollars on a note to Strome which I would sign?"

He made no reply for a moment to this extraordinary suggestion, but thought a minute, looking off into space.

"I have to go to Salt Lake this afternoon," he said

presently, "and I'll take the matter up down there. Come in in the morning and I'll let you know."

I left the bank and went to find Doty who had been so worried that I didn't want to be with him. Young's mention of Salt Lake City was too much for me. Little known as I was in Ogden, I was known by fewer still in Salt Lake. And then, quite suddenly, I began to see the light. Young might go to Salt Lake City, but he'd learn little enough about me there. He would wire Omaha without a doubt.

I took a long breath. I might get that eighteen thousand dollars after all.

Doty and I were staying at the Depot Hotel, and Doty, I remember, did not go to bed at all that night. He sat in the lobby and walked the streets by turns, as worried as any man I ever saw, certain that no one could get money in quantities such as we required it from men we did not know, and certain, too, that such danger as no man would care to have his family face hung over his as they awaited our return there in that Indian Creek camp.

I worried, too, naturally, though I got to sleep. Very early I was awake, however, and walking the streets with Doty. It seemed to both of us that nine o'clock would never come. How long the hours were that morning, and how blank were the drawn shades of the First National Bank of Ogden!

Finally, however, the shades went up, and the bank was opened. I entered at once, and asked if Mr. Young was there. I was directed to the open door of his office. He saw me as I approached and asked me in.

"The bank," he said at once, "can make you that loan."

"How about Strome?" I asked.

"That will be acceptable," he replied.

I thanked him and went at once for Strome. When I had brought him back Young himself filled out the notes and gave them to us to sign, and then and there I obtained the money, but the interest rate, I very distinctly recall, was two per cent a month.

I never bothered about those notes again. Strome looked out for that, and years later he sent the canceled notes to me as souvenirs. I have them yet.

Doty and I were ready now to go back to our camp on Indian Creek, but having gone into Strome's office about something else, I was leaving again when I heard a door open behind me, and heard my name called.

I turned about to see an acquaintance by the name of Bancroft standing there. He was from Omaha and a member of the firm of Wood & Bancroft, railroad contractors.

"Mr. Kimball will be in Denver tomorrow," he said in a low voice, and backed through the door, closing it in my face.

I stood there puzzled. That whole trip to Ogden had been a sort of mystery, and I had been surmising and guessing and wondering ever since I had arrived. And now here was something else to make me wonder. I wondered whether to go and ask Bancroft what he had meant, but decided not to. He was not given to talking in circles, and undoubtedly he had said all he intended to say. And yet, why had he told me that? I thought about it for an hour, and finally decided that something lay behind it, and that I would be in Denver tomorrow as well.

I sent Doty off with the borrowed money, therefore, and took the train for Denver myself.

I boarded the train fifteen minutes or so before it left, and was seated in the Pullman when I heard some familiar voices. Looking up, I saw Corrigan and his partner Carlisle, and with them were Dave Kilpatrick and Collins, a nephew of Sydney Dillon and, in some way never entirely clear to me, Dillon's representative in much of the railroad building that was so energetically being furthered in the West by Sydney Dillon and Jay Gould.

Collins and Kilpatrick were associated, too, in the contracting firm of Kilpatrick Brothers and Collins, the largest and most powerful firm, with the possible exception of Corrigan and Carlisle, that was at work on the Dillon-Gould enterprise.

"Ho!" shouted one of them as he saw me. "Look who's here. Where are *you* going?"

I did not exactly know, for while Denver was my destination I had no clear idea of just what I would find there.

"Oh," I replied, "we're cleaning up up there on the Indian Creek, and I'm just going off to get a little rest."

They seemed to take me at my word, and went off through the train to their own accommodations. Throughout the trip they seemed inclined to keep to themselves, and I made no effort to intrude. That their business and mine—whatever mine should prove to be—were somehow connected, I did not doubt, but I preferred to talk to Mr. Kimball before I did anything else.

Asking at the Denver depot the next morning where I would find Kimball, I was told that his private car was in the yard. When I went there, however, I was told that he had gone to the office of Mr. Stanton, a railroad official in charge of much of the engineering work.

Going to Stanton's office, I asked for Kimball, and was told that he was out but would be in again presently. I had not long to wait when he came in. He greeted me with no surprise, and took me into the office he was using.

"What are your relations," he asked, "with the Kilpatrick Brothers?"

"Oh, we're friendly," I replied, "but I have never done any business with them."

He nodded.

"We have some work to do," he said, "on the Denver, South Park, and Pacific, at Buena Vista, and we can give it to you. This afternoon you go up to Major Evans' office, and he'll have a contract for you."

I left him, very well pleased with my prospects. My work on the Oregon Short Line would soon be finished—it was a matter of weeks, now—and here was something that would take my enlarged outfit at once. That afternoon, therefore, I did as Kimball had instructed me to do, and found a contract awaiting me. Then I learned, too, what connection Collins had with it. His relations with Dillon had obtained for Kilpatrick Brothers and Collins this contract that now was given to me, together with a much larger contract for a line to Leadville. The latter contract had now been split between his firm and Corrigan and Carlisle, while the contract for the work at Buena Vista, with Collins' signature upon it, had—at Kimball's suggestion, I believe—been given to me.

"And it's at the same figure that Collins got it for," Major Evans explained.

I was pleased, you can be sure. The two firms that had been represented on the train from Ogden were quite the most powerful in the field in which my smaller outfit was working. It was pleasant to realize that they had not squeezed me out, and I went back to the camp on Indian Creek with the firm belief that my affairs were about to show improvement.

9

THE ROUGHNESS of the Idaho of the eighties can hardly be exaggerated, and the toughness of many of the men with whom we came in almost daily contact certainly can't. Because of the number of these bad men, Bob Kilpatrick of Kilpatrick Brothers and Collins, never went anywhere without his bodyguard—a swarthy, black-haired, black-eyed Mexican who invariably trailed behind Bob and who always wore a heavy cartridge belt from which hung two loaded holsters.

The Kilpatrick camp was among the largest in that country, and being large, had more tough men about it than smaller camps like mine. I had been in the Kilpatrick camps often, for there were many things to learn there. One thing I observed, however, which I did not imitate.

One big cook tent in the Kilpatrick camp supplied food for several dining tents, in each of which several long tables stood—tables with boards along each side to serve as seats. Entering one of these one day just after the noonday meal I saw the tin plates spaced with such extraordinary precision about the tables as to arouse my interest. After a meal in my camp the tables looked as if a hurricane had just passed through, but here in the Kilpatrick camp the plates were still placed with such extraordinary accuracy as to suggest the use of a chalk line and ruler.

My next glance showed me plainly that the plates held the remains of the meal that had been served, and then, to my amazement, a man appeared with a pail of water and a stick with a rag fastened to its end. He soused the swab into his pail and swabbed out a plate or two, and sousing the swab again, continued down one side of the table, giving each tin plate a lick and a promise.

My interest was now well aroused, and I looked more closely, for never had I seen such cleaning up as that before. And, too, I was amazed at the man's ability to swab out a tin plate, which is a very easily moved object, without moving it a fraction of an inch from the place it occupied on the table.

But suddenly as I approached a table and looked down into a swabbed-out plate on which the wet and dirty rag had left a spiral pattern of food particles, I saw the reason. Every one of those scores and scores of tin plates was nailed securely through its bottom to the table.

"What in the name of common sense—" I began, and the man with the swab stopped.

"Huh?" he grunted, obviously asking me what I was driving at.

"Why, what have you got these plates nailed down for?" I asked.

"So's we kin git more men at each table," he explained. "If we don't nail 'em down they'll pile one plate on another and take up too much room. This way we kin crowd 'em in."

And crowd them in they did, for those plates were spaced so closely together that they left very little room for elbow work. The swabbing process, too, was not the method of cleaning up before the plates were washed. That was all the washing those plates ever got.

The work all along the Oregon Short Line was progressing rapidly by now, and most of the construction work from American Falls to the junction with the O. R. & N. was finished. Track was laid to a little beyond Cañon Creek, which lies not far west of the town of Mountain Home, and passenger trains were operating as far as Shoshone. Beyond there, to the end of track, nothing but supply trains for the construction work were as yet being operated. My camp was, however, nine hard hours' drive to the west and north of the end of track.

So nearly completed was the work that, aside from the bridge gangs and the gang engaged in laying the track, there were no big payrolls left except that of Kilpatrick Brothers and Collins and my own. A few contractors had not yet shipped out their outfits, but their work was done, and every highwayman and holdup man in all that region had only a very few payrolls to think about and try to get. Such holdups had been very profitable for these gunmen, and the time was coming within a few weeks when there would be no more such opportunities. The golden hay must therefore be made while the setting sun still shone.

The country was literally filled with money, for wages had been high, and every workman had gold pieces to clink together in his pocket. How hard those fellows labored, though, to get it! And yet how willing they were to risk it at cards. I remember seeing two teamsters of mine sitting on the ground one day when they had stopped work to feed their horses. Between them was a bag of oats, and they were busily engaged in doing something on it.

"What the dognation are you fellows up to?" I called out from a little distance off.

One of them looked up and grinned.

"Aw, Bill here says he can play seven-up," he explained, "and I'm just a-bettin' him twenty dollars he can't."

They each dropped a twenty-dollar gold piece on their improvised table, and the game began with a pack of greasy cards that one of them pulled from his overalls pocket.

By great good fortune no saloon tent ever appeared at our camp on Indian Creek. Perhaps it was because of the stick of dynamite with which I had driven the liquor dealer away from the Wood River camp. That story was public property, of course, and it may be that no one else in the business cared for dynamite. But whatever the reason, they did not come. And Boise, the nearest town, was too far off for the men to get there often. Gamblers, however, were numerous enough. Contracting camps being so limited now, it was easy to get men, but because it was only men who were working who had money, it was natural that gamblers would come in. They would get their names on the time book and pretend to work, and then—usually operating in pairs—they would get the men into poker games in the evenings and on Sundays, fleecing them by every means known to the gambler's shady art. These gamblers, too, were the very kind of gentry who kept the bands of highwaymen informed when any payrolls or money transfers were to be found upon the road.

The work was going fast, and I was forever having to

go out upon the road in order to hurry up the freighters who were always on the way from Shoshone—about one hundred and twenty-five miles—with supplies. On the way to camp there was a very steep section of road at King Hill, where the tons of freight sometimes made trouble for the teams. The grade was very steep and very long—so bad, in fact, that the brakes would often fail. I have seen trees along that trail almost cut in two by the ropes used by the freighters in snubbing their loaded wagons down. Our stuff came up, of course, which was harder, and King Hill was always a good place to look for delayed freighting outfits. There was a deserted house at the foot of the hill, and once, arriving there after dark and looking for a place to put down my bedding roll, I found a little structure eight or ten feet square, and lighting a match, spread my blankets and tried to go to sleep. Something, however, was crawling over me, and I couldn't sleep. I finally lighted another match, and looking closely found the place to be literally alive with what I imagine were chicken lice, the structure having evidently once been a chicken coop. I made no further effort to remain, but hauled my blankets outside. There I undressed, and stood naked and shivering in the dark, shaking my blankets and my clothes as vigorously as I could to rid them of that vermin. I succeeded fairly well, too, and finally made my bed again beside an old, old stack of musty hay where I finally warmed up enough to sleep.

The high dry plains of Idaho were extraordinarily hot almost every day in summer, the thermometer often registering one hundred and twenty degrees. So dry was the air, however, that horses, working hard at the heavy work of loading scrapers, seemed never to sweat enough to wet a hair.

The nights, by contrast, were cold. In the morning, following a day when the thermometer had gone far past the hundred-mark, I have often found a thin coating of ice on the water pail that always sat beneath the fly of my tent, and by throwing a double blanket over the pail, I have kept the water cool all day. By midday, however, or early afternoon, the surface of the ground would be so hot that the dogs would whimper, picking up their feet as if on coals. Often I've seen teamsters stop and lift their dogs into the wagons because the poor beasts could no longer stand the heat of the parched earth. If a person stopped, too, for more than a few seconds, he'd have to kick away the soil in order to get his feet below that thin, overheated surface layer which was scorched too hot to permit one's standing still.

It took tough and hardy men to stay in such a land—or great determination. It is no wonder that so many "ring-tailed roarers" were about and that gentleness and consideration were things almost unknown. Thick skins, brute force, and constant determination were almost essential, and they were common enough attributes about our camps in those days. Quarreling, wasting, stealing, gambling, the men out there still managed to work as well. Profanity was so prevalent as quite to lose its force. Hardly a remark but contained great strings of expletives. But work was still the order of the day—hard work, such as men have rarely done.

We came at last to the end of it. Only a few remaining touches were still ahead of our men to do. The final inspection was made by the engineers, and now we had only to pay off our men and ship that greatly enlarged outfit back to Colorado. And yet the problem was not so simple as it sounds.

The payroll had grown enormously. It would take the better part of twenty thousand dollars to pay the men for that last month, and bad men from all over the United States and Mexico were in the country. Where formerly they had been scattered along two hundred and fifty miles or so of railroad right of way, now, because so much had been completed, they were largely congregated in a very much restricted district.

It was inconceivable that any payroll could be brought in secretly enough to keep those gunmen from knowing it was due. It only remained to try to dodge them, and failing that, to fight it out or turn the money over. The prospect was not pleasant, but one could not blink it. To Ogden I had to go—and with Stitt, my bookkeeper, too, in order that his records could be examined. He was not a timid soul, of course, for timid folk were scarce out there. But he was a bookkeeper, not a wielder of six-shooters. I had no confidence in him if it came to pulling triggers. I do not mean any of this as a reflection on Stitt, for a more faithful, devoted man never worked for me. But guns were not for him.

Still, he had to go, and Doty, too, who was a kind of partner on that work, must go as well, which did not strengthen the party much. Doty was a good man at moving dirt—or rather at making the men move it—but he was nervous and far from handy with a gun. He had, it is true, brought in that borrowed eighteen thousand dollars the month before, but I was as much afraid of Doty's shooting as of anyone's, and began to see what Nichols had had in mind when he had told me he didn't want my help that day on the depot platform at Shoshone.

I looked a little further, therefore, not wanting a bodyguard, exactly, but more than willing to have some fellow with me whose nerve and aim were steady enough to be of service if a test of them should come. Nor, in a camp like that, did I have very far to look. Frank Luddington was still working with me as a subcontractor, and I spoke to him. It wasn't necessary to enlarge on the problem, for he knew the situation better, if anything, than I did.

"Lud," I said, "I've got to go to Ogden with Doty and Stitt, and I'd like to have you come back with us."

He nodded.

"Sure, I'll go," he agreed, and it was not necessary to discuss it much. He had done such things before, and had a sawed-off shotgun that he carried on such errands, its walnut stock tucked up under his right arm. I got him a round-trip pass, I remember, and having some affairs of his own in Ogden, he went off a day or two ahead of us.

Doty, Stitt, and I left camp in my buckboard, with Jim, a pacer, and Frank, a trotter, hitched to it, and nine or ten hours later arrived at end of track. There was, of course, no town there, but men were constantly going and coming, with the result that a kind of tent village had been set up. A couple of men had set up a business with two tents—one a stable tent, where horses were stabled for their absent owners, and the other a "bunkhouse" or "flophouse" where, within the confines of the walls of the big tents, the sagebrush and the cactus had been cleared away so that men could spread their bedrolls on the ground. There was a charge of one dollar for that privilege, but I have forgotten what fantastic figure was set upon the "stabling" of horses in the stable tent. However, we left the team and horses there, climbing aboard the caboose of an empty construction train that was heading back to Shoshone.

Hundreds of men had seen us drive away from camp, and the departure of the bookkeeper fairly shouted that we were going for the final settlement, especially as payday was only four days off. We knew all that, but all we could do was to go, trying to figure out some method of dodging a holdup on our return.

We reached Ogden in the evening, and registered at the Depot Hotel. This hostelry, at which all railroad employees obtained a special rate, stood not far from where the Utah Northern crossed the Union Pacific, a good half mile from the business section of the town. We met Luddington there, and immediately after breakfast all of us went down to the disbursing office on the second floor of the building next door to the bank of Guthrie, Dooly, and Company.

Strome, the disbursing clerk, had been expecting us, and the estimate, with the final check pinned fast to it, was waiting. The necessary accounting was simple, for Stitt had all the figures and reports, and within a few minutes Strome had recorded what he needed and handed the check to me—a check for a little over twenty-three thousand six hundred dollars.

It was by now hardly more than nine o'clock, and a train for Pocatello was due to leave within the hour. We went at once to Guthrie, Dooly, and Company, therefore, on whom the check was drawn, and going to the window I presented the check to none other than Mr. Dooly himself, for he stood behind the wicket.

He did not speak to me as I approached; that blistering I had given him still rankled I suppose. Instead, with a face as expressionless as a pan of dough, he looked at the check, examined my endorsement, and putting it aside, swung open the wicket, stooped down and lifted, one at a time, four canvas bags of gold, on each of which was stamped five thousand dollars.

"Oh Mr. Dooly," I began. "Don't give me that. We have to carry this money a long way. Let me have it in currency."

He stood back with his hands upon the shelf before him, still with no expression in his face, and with his eyes on those canvas bags.

"That's a legal tender, sir," he replied, clipping his words off short.

I saw I could do nothing, and train time was near.

"Well," I went on, "let me have the six hundred-odd in dollars, halves, and quarters."

We had to have that much change, despite its weight, and he handed it out in rolls, finally placing the remaining three thousand dollars which he paid, for a wonder, in currency, on the pile, dropping a folded canvas "treasury" sack on top of it.

I handed one of the bags to each of my companions, stuffed the currency into my inside coat pocket, dropped the fourth bag of gold and all the silver into the "treasury" sack, and off we went.

The other three, each with his bag of gold upon his shoulder, walked along readily enough, but having shouldered that weighty sack of gold and silver and swung it over my back, I needed help long before we had walked the rather considerable distance to the station. Luddington traded with me, finally, and we reached the station only a little before the train backed in. Had we had more time we could no doubt have exchanged that gold at some other bank for the currency that Dooley refused to give me, but we were anxious to get back to camp, for the sooner we completed that round trip the more unexpected our return would be.

Having boarded the train, however, we began to worry. We did not take a Pullman—perhaps there was no Pullman on the train—but rode instead in a day coach the one hundred and twenty miles to Pocatello. There, by a stroke of luck, we had to shoulder our golden burdens and run down the tracks in order to catch a loaded construction train that was starting at once for the end of track. Our luck so far was good, for had we taken a passenger train to Shoshone we could not have failed to parade the station platform there with all that money in plain sight. As it was we rode in the construction train caboose—the only passengers—and none of Pinkston's hangers-on got a glimpse of those canvas bags when, finally, we rattled slowly through Shoshone, and out over the rough roadbed that lay beyond it, to where, just over Cañon Creek, our buckboard and horses were waiting in the stable tent.

Never in my life before or since have I been so keyed up. All the way from Ogden my every sense was sharply alert, and Luddington, too, was watching. What was going on in Doty's mind or Stitt's I do not know, but neither of them had any hankering for what still lay ahead. Doty's trip with the eighteen thousand dollars had been different. He had the money, it is true, but it had not been in evidence. Nor had he been accustomd to carrying the payroll, for that had been a job that I had kept. His trip had not been without its possible dangers, it is true, but this that we were taking now was worse. Hundreds of men in Ogden had seen us with that gold. Scores more at Pocatello had seen us just as plainly, and telegrams of seeming innocence could so easily have carried the news ahead. Nor did it need to be carried at all. The poorest fool in camp knew what we had gone for, and the gamblers and gunmen there were certainly not fools. But then, that construction train from Pocatello had helped. It was not likely that any hangers-on at camp would think of our taking it, even if they had known, which was unlikely, that it was coming.

The possibility of our being held up on the train had kept us wary, of course, but we knew the danger was not greatest there. What I was thoroughly convinced of—what I positively *knew*—was that somewhere between the end of track and camp they would attempt to take that money from us. And I was rigidly determined to shoot it out when they should come. Only a few months back I had been sixty-three thousand dollars in debt—all but ruined—and now, after working and struggling as I had never thought I could, I had paid those debts except for the payroll I had still to meet. Once that was paid I would be clear again—clear and with my outfit larger by far than it had ever been—clear with some thousands of that money we were carrying mine—mine, by Heaven! —and a contract still ahead that with care would establish me on firmer ground.

The construction train rattled and bumped to a stop at the end of track just after the sun had set, and instantly we shouldered our money and strode off toward the stable tent, beside which, in the dusk, we saw my buckboard standing.

"Doty," I ordered, as we put the money in, "you go off over there and cut me an armful of willow branches. I haven't got a whip. Lud, you get the horses. Stitt and I will wait."

They hurried off, and Stitt suggested that we get a

bite to eat at an eating place in a tent not far off. I would not hear of it. We had a nine-hour drive ahead and I proposed to make it in less if possible. No wasting time with food just now. Our horses were well fed, and that was all we needed.

Doty came back with the willow branches and Lud led out the horses. The neckyoke and the traces were hooked in place and we climbed in—Doty on my left as I took the reins, Stitt on the low slat bed of the buckboard with his feet hanging off behind, Lud, with his sawed-off shotgun, beside Stitt and behind me.

"Now listen," I began. "The minute I see 'em coming I'll start shooting. And if it's a bunch I'm going to make 'em all get off the trail to the east. I'm not going to let 'em separate. And Doty, when I start shooting, you keep out of my way. Dive off into the sagebrush if you want to, but don't get in front of me or you'll get shot. And Lud, I expect you to stay with me."

"By God, old man," he replied, "I will."

"But if you start using that shotgun," I insisted, "you get off the buckboard. Don't shoot past me. Get off and get out to the side."

He agreed, and I tightened the reins.

"Now, remember," I went on, keyed up to such a pitch as I had never been before, "if this money don't reach camp, it'll be because I'm dead!"

I took one of Doty's willow branches and began then and there upon those willing horses. Out across the plains toward the fading sunset we started, with more than twenty thousand dollars there beneath Doty's feet and mine—with three thousand more in my coat pocket—and with the barrel of my .44 beneath my thigh, its butt turned up where I could grasp it quickly. We drove three miles or four before darkness came, the narrow wheels of the buckboard inches deep in sand, lifting it with every turn and pouring it in steady streams on Stitt and Luddington.

The tents at the end of track faded away behind us, and slowly the details of sagebrush and greasewood faded in the coming dark. The horses, on whom I constantly used that willow branch, were settling into their stride—Jim swinging a little from side to side as he paced through the sand—Frank's trotting feet almost noiseless on the trail. Now and then we jolted and rattled over a patch of rock, or jerked and bumped across a gully. Off to the left lay the graded right of way, no tracks as yet upon it, and after awhile, having struck a rougher stretch, I turned the horses toward it, and drove up a two-foot fill, turning along the level grade.

Now and again we came to places where bridges would be built to span some dry creek bed or other, and down we went to rattle through the gullies, bouncing and careening up beyond them to get upon the grade again.

These breaks in the level right of way grew more frequent and in the dark we all but overturned in crossing one. Such traveling was too slow, and back I went to the sandy trail once more, to urge the horses on and sift more sand on Stitt and Lud.

I strained my eyes and watched the faint horizon there ahead. The sky was dark, but the earth lay darker still, and there against that faint horizon I knew that any instant I might see the silhouettes of horsemen. Broken, wind-deformed sagebrush now and then seemed to be men, and my hand fell to my upturned revolver butt. Time after time I almost raised that gun. Time after time I released the butt and raised my hand to the reins again.

I wore a willow branch to shreds, and throwing it away I took another from Doty who sat silently beside me. We said little—almost nothing—expecting any moment to hear the sound of shots.

Stitt scratched a match to see what time it was. I swore at him. A match in the clear air on that level plain might be seen a mile.

Mile after mile rolled past. Hour after hour. All of us were smokers, but we smoked nothing now, and almost constantly I used the willow branches on both Jim and Frank and stared through the night at the horizon ahead. Up over the undulations of the plain we rattled, staring down into the darkness of the lower land ahead. Down we rattled into the shallow hollows, searching the horizon for the shapes we knew were somewhere between us there in that vast desert and the camp long miles ahead.

I sat tensely upright in the seat, leaning forward a little, unsupported by the back, always conscious of the heavy butt of my revolver there between my legs.

To a person riding in the seat of a buckboard it is a reasonably comfortable conveyance, for the long, tough wooden slats upon which the seat is placed are resilient enough to take up much of the roughness of the road, and the springs beneath the seat take up still more. But Stitt and Lud, there upon those slats behind, had no such help to make their ride more comfortable. The thin ash boards barely separated them from the light hind axle. The sand poured down upon them from the wheels and every jar and jolt came to them with force enough, it must have seemed, to drive their spinal columns through their very skulls.

Their feet, too, swung down behind, for there was no place else to put them, and furthermore, my opening shots would be the first announcement that the holdup men had come. It speaks whole worlds for Lud that I could count securely on his steady nerves. Yet count I did.

More miles and more. More hours and still more hours. Still those horses kept their stride—Jim still pacing—Frank still holding to his trot. I took the last of Doty's willow branches, and on we went through the darkness and the night.

Another hour, and in the east the sky turned very faintly grey. We swayed and bounced across a gully that I knew—a small one, but a welcome one, for it was close to camp. The grade rose gradually, and now a hundred yards away, I saw the ghostly shapes of silent tents, grey and huddled in the silent, faintly greying night. The commissary tent stood there ahead, the faint light of a lamp within showing weakly through the canvas. I pulled up the horses before its entrance, and stiffly we alighted. Without a word we pulled out our load of gold and moving almost painfully, carried it toward where the canvas flap hung motionless across the entrance.

As we reached it the canvas drew back suddenly, and there stood Crowe, looking keenly at us.

"What are you up so early for?" I asked.

He beckoned us in.

"I've been up all night," he replied.

"What for?"

He raised his finger.

"Come here," he ordered.

We crossed the tent to its side wall. He pulled the loose wall down an inch or two and pointed out. I stared out in the faint, faint light, and there beside a tent not thirty feet away, five horses stood—their saddles and their bridles on.

"Hmph," I grunted. "What are they doing?"

"Perhaps they thought you wouldn't be in so soon," he whispered. "Anyway they got up a poker game. One of our men got roped into it and came to me for some money. He told me they were playing, and I didn't try to stop 'em, you can bet."

I took a long breath.

"Don't charge it up to him," I said, and sat down weakly on a trunk. Where Lud and Stitt and Doty went I do not know. I went to sleep there on that trunk, and didn't awake for hours.

10

IT WOULD be difficult to imagine greater changes in any land than those that have taken place in Idaho since the early eighties. Where we struggled and labored in that parched and sagebrush-covered desert, orchards bloom today. Where not a village—hardly a structure of any kind—stood between Mountain Home and Nampa, now pleasant towns lie all along the railroad that we built. In a land devoid of water, save as here and there one found a stream, now irrigation ditches have turned the desert dust into fruitful soil.

It may seem hard to believe that I fed my men on venison until they turned against it. Frank Coran of my outfit proposed shooting deer for food. I bought him a rifle, therefore, and paid him three cents a pound for what we used. At first we purchased the whole of the cleaned carcasses, but they were too numerous and we soon bought only the hindquarters, or saddles. During the winter of 1882-83 Frank delivered about two hundred and fifty deer at our cook tent. The deer were easy to get, for as cold weather came they left the higher land about the Sawtooth Mountains and dropped down into the valley of Wood River.

Trout, too, were endlessly plentiful—fine Rocky Mountain trout, speckled brown. On one occasion, a group of men, armed with fuses, caps, and dynamite, took a team of light mules and a wagon after trout. I saw them coming back to camp, the wagon wheels running deep in sand. The men were walking, and the mules were working hard to pull the load. About a thousand pounds of trout were in the wagon—fine big fellows that seemed to me, as I looked over the wagon's tailboard, to average over a foot in length. We had many wagonloads of trout from Wood River, but never another one so heavily laden as that. The supply in that first wagon was too generous, and after that they brought back fewer.

Since those days I have heard much criticism of the destruction of fish and game of which we and others, both earlier and later, were guilty. The most that I can say for the criticism is that it is based upon the easy wisdom of hindsight. In a land so sparsely populated by people and so rich in game as was Idaho in those days, it was inconceivable to any of us that the wild life could ever come so near being exterminated. As far as I saw, there were few "game hogs." What we took, we used. When, for instance, we purchased only the saddles of the deer Frank Coran killed, he found a market for the rest—at a lower figure than our three cents a pound, of course. Were I faced with a similar situation today I would realize the danger, and I hope that I would act accordingly. But I feel certain that unless the law should take a hand, there are many men today who would think far less of the future of the wild life than of the pleasure of bagging as many fish and fowl and deer and antelope as their time and energy would permit. Perhaps both we and the "game hogs" of a later day were criminals, but if so, I feel reasonably confident that we were the less depraved.

There were, of course, other wild inhabitants of the region less acceptable than the fish and game—rattlesnakes, for instance. They were almost everywhere, and on one occasion a man gave me a large cigar box full of rattles he had taken from snakes that he had killed. Yet strangely enough, in all the time we worked there not a man or horse was bitten in my camp. The buzzing rattle of the snakes was a common sound, and the men were forever killing them, yet they did no harm. I never so much as killed one, though I've walked out of my way to avoid them a thousand times, I'm sure.

Tarantulas, though not the great black fellows one sees in the tropics, and scorpions were far from rare, and we ultimately learned to laugh at scorpion stings as if they were no worse than bees. I saw a scorpion sting a man on the back of his neck, but the fellow merely swore and brushed the thing away, resuming his conversation when he had set his foot upon it.

Horned toads and good-sized lizards that we called "swifts" were not uncommon, and I have never seen a more rapidly moving creature than a "swift." The name must certainly have come to them because of their rapid movement. But of all the smaller denizens of the plains of Idaho the kangaroo rats appealed to me the most. Caught and brought to camp, they became tame almost immediately, and almost always we had one about the commissary, and someone gave me one to keep about my tent. I even took one of the odd little big-eyed, long-tailed things to the home I had, by now, built in Omaha.

One of the oddest bits of the natural history of the Idaho I knew were the enormous armies of black crickets that sometimes were to be seen moving across the country. On one occasion I saw a vast black carpet of those insects crossing a road, and drove my team through them. How far they stretched from where they were coming from to wherever they were going I do not know, but the army was between three and four hundred feet wide where I crossed it, and they were crowded so thickly together that I could not see the earth beneath them.

The Old Oregon Trail crossed Idaho, of course, and it must not be thought that because the railroad reached the coast the trail was no longer in use. On a trip to western Nebraska, very near the Wyoming line, I once saw the emigrants on the trail in the eighties, and from where I pulled my team out to the side of the many trails that made up that historic route, I could see an almost unbroken stream of emigrants from horizon to horizon—a distance of not less than eight miles or ten. Teams and covered wagons, horsemen, little bunches of cows, more wagons, some drawn by cows, men walking, women and children riding—an endless stream of hardy, optimistic folk, going west to seek their fortunes and to settle an empire.

We saw so much of things like that that we thought nothing of it. It was the order of the day, and had been going on for years. But there in Idaho I saw another phase of the old trail that led to Oregon. Riding along it not far from American Falls, I came upon an old, old group of graves, and stopped. There were the neatly arranged piles of lava rock piled on those graves to protect the bodies buried there from wolves and coyotes. Wooden headboards, worn by blowing sand, stood or lay at each of them. The constant blowing of the sand had worn some of the boards to paper thinness near the ground, and finally the wind had blown them down. Some kindly person had re-erected some of these, and propped them up with stone. But there was one that stood taller than the rest, still as it had been left by the person who had erected it. It was made, it seemed, from the heavy board side of a wagon box, and upon its sturdy surface which, save near the ground where the sand had worn it thin, was clear, I read a woman's name. I have forgotten now what name it was, but under it was carved "and child." Below that was the day and month, and 1855 stood at the bottom.

What care the man who had carved that board had taken with it! What heartbreak there was written there, plain in the delicate perfection of that lettering! Tears almost came to my eyes as I thought of that woman and her child, and of the man who left them there in that vast desert—left them there and journeyed on to play his part in settling up the West.

We paid off our men at Indian Creek, and then broke camp. Every bill I owed was paid. I even sent the necessary money home to make the final payment on the house my wife and I had built. My outfit was greatly larger than it had ever been, and I had four thousand dollars cash beside. Not bad, I thought, after having been sixty-three thousand dollars in debt hardly six months before.

And now we packed our wagons and set off for the end of track where a train of boxcars and a coach awaited us. It took thirty-one cars to carry that outfit of mine, and you can believe that I was proud of it. Horses, harness, wagons, scrapers, tools, tents, and cases of supplies. The coach was for the men I took, for I needed more than a few to look after such a trainload.

The Denver, South Park, & Pacific was a narrow-gauge railroad, which was anything but unusual in those days. Even the Denver & Rio Grande was narrow gauge, for railroad men felt uncertain of their ability to run standard gauge lines through the mountains and the gorges. At Denver, consequently, my outfit was transferred to narrow-gauge cars, and when we started on again, *two* trains were required to haul it.

Buena Vista lies roughly midway between the Royal Gorge and Leadville, where the D. S. P. & P. crossed the D. & R. G., and it was a relief to find myself at such a pleasant place after those awful plains of Idaho. The town was small, but it had a nice two-story frame hotel, called the Lake House, across the tracks from the railroad station—and had, as well, real stores and harness shops and all the rest, including the inevitable saloons.

The work we were to do was about two miles from town, and tired of living in a tent, I took a room at the Lake House and stabled my horses at a livery stable within half a block of the place. Down the street past the two-story brick courthouse the road to camp led very directly, and I grew to know that road right well before I finished.

Not far beyond the courthouse a field beside the road was piled with vast boulders. Across the road the scrub cedar grew thick, solidly covering the slope. Beyond this, in the valley, lay a part of the work we were to do, and looking down upon us was that amazingly beautiful Collegiate Range, a sight to make one stop at any time, but especially in the autumn.

I often saw the tips of that bold range swathed in swirling snow, while not so far below the eddying snow the frosted leaves of the aspens glowed like gold. Farther down the mountain side the mountain oak was red, and lower still the blue spruce stood like haze upon the slope. Then came the piñon pines and finally the ranches, with patches of color all their own to make the foreground of the picture. A score of times I've stopped my horses to stare. There hung that gorgeous tapestry of nature—fifty miles long and ten miles wide —its lower edge before my very horses, and its top among the clouds.

There were, of course, saloons and gamblers there in town, but I congratulated myself at being back in civilization once again, and enjoyed it to the full. There were, however, a few flies in the ointment, for some gamblers, sensing easy money with a railroad outfit there, blew into town. Still, I did not know them, and thought but little of it until one of them—a fellow by the name of Barns—together with a hanger-on, took to riding their horses up and down the main street "shooting up the town." They rode into saloons and shot through the ceilings, and even rode into a dry goods store and did the same thing there.

It disgusted me, as it did many of the people of the town, but I was more disgusted later when I asked the keeper of the livery stable about it. He, being the mayor of the town, had some responsibility in the matter, but he failed to rise to it.

"Why the devil don't you arrest this fellow?" I demanded of him one day.

"Oh," replied the mayor, "he's a bad man when he's in liquor. I'm afraid if we tried to arrest him he'd kill somebody. But he's all right when he ain't drunk, and anyway, he can't last long, a-drinkin' like he is."

"But he's liable to hurt somebody," I objected.

"Oh no," replied the mayor. "He's a good shot."

I came in to the hotel late one afternoon, after a particularly hard day on the work, and immediately after supper I went to bed. I had had some trouble getting a gang of Mexicans to do their work, and I was worn out. I went to sleep at once and sometime later—but I don't remember the hour—I was awakened by a terrific racket in the corridor on both sides of which the rooms were located. Someone was out there shouting and pounding on doors, yelling for people to come out so that he could beat them up.

I was tired, as I have said, and wanted to sleep, but with that unearthly racket going on I couldn't, so I merely lay there, growing more and more angry with every passing moment. I had hoped that the noise would cease, but it did not. It increased, rather, for whoever was responsible for it was coming toward my room, pounding on every intervening door as he did so. And finally he reached mine.

He kicked the door until it rattled.

"Come out of there, you —— —— —— —— ——!" he roared.

I have been angry in my time, but never, I believe, as angry as I was then. I was undressed, of course, and clad only in my nightshirt, with my artificial leg lying on a chair. I swung out of bed, picking up my .44 as I did so, and hopping around the bed I took hold of the doorknob with my left hand.

Never before or since have I had firmly in my mind the clear intention of shooting a man, but I had at that moment. I was going to pull that door open and shoot the shouting idiot directly in the face. I raised my gun, turned the knob, and pulled.

There, almost in the open door, stood Barns, the

gambler, but the instant my eyes fell upon him I knew I could not shoot. He was roaring drunk, and was dressed only in a suit of red underwear.

I did not pull the trigger, but the heavy gun came down. So close was he to me that he was well within my reach, and I brought the heavy barrel of that .44 down on his head. Twice I struck him, and he crumpled at my feet. He was partially bald, I remember, and the gun did its work effectively, but he had barely fallen, with his roaring temporarily silenced, when up the stairs his favorite hanger-on came running.

The stairs reached the second-story corridor within ten feet of my door, and he no sooner appeared than I covered him.

"Put 'em up!" I roared. "Put 'em up!" and loosed a string of my own choicest profanity at him.

He put them up, too.

"Now lie down on your back, you dirty pup," I yelled, "and put up your feet!"

He did that, too, and as he lay there, his hands and feet in the air, I heard the sound of running feet upon the stairs. In another moment the chief of police and two of his officers were there. The cowardly fellows had been in the lobby all the while, and never until that moment had they made a move.

I lit into them, of course.

"Now take these fellows out," I ordered, when I had let loose a few of my opinions, "and lock 'em up. Somebody's got to run this town and keep it decent, and if you can't do it there are men who can."

The chief did not reply, nor did his men, but collared the two and led them off, while I went back to bed.

I was so furious, however, and so worked up that

I could not sleep. Barns had still been lying on the floor when the police had reached him, and I did not know how badly he was hurt. I might have cracked his fool skull, for all I knew, and it bothered me. I had no desire to kill a man.

I got up finally and dressed, going down into the lobby to learn just how badly I had hurt him. There was quite a group of men there. I asked how much Barns had been hurt.

"Oh, not much," someone replied. "His head was cut, but a doctor sewed him up and put some sticking plaster on it. He's in jail."

I would have asked more, but more men were coming in, gawking at me as at a freak in a side show, so off I went to bed again, and finally got to sleep. It was not until late the next morning that I awoke, and when I went down I found the dining room door closed. The clerk, however, saw my hesitation, and told me to go in—that they would serve me.

In the dining room I had made it a habit to sit at the second table on the right of the door as one entered, and as I went in that morning two men were sitting there, their backs toward me, while a third had pulled a chair out from the first table and sat nonchalantly behind them. I thought nothing of it, and went to my accustomed place and sat down before I looked at them. I started when I did, however, for there were Barns and his partner glumly eating breakfast, with the guard who had brought them over from jail sitting behind them. Barns's thin face was serious enough and his mustache was moving a little as he chewed, while on his head a big white cross of sticking plaster marked the place where my gun had struck.

What might happen I did not know, but I intended to be ready, so I moved over to the side of my chair and tucked my coattail back so as to be able quickly to pull my .44 from my hip pocket if I needed to.

No one made a move, however, and they finished breakfast just before I did, leaving the dining room and heading back to jail as I pushed back my chair.

There was much talk about the affair, but I considered the incident closed, and being busy, gave my mind to other things. Not long thereafter, however, we paid our men, and a faithful, simple-minded Swede named Pete Larsen, whom I had had in Idaho, was fool enough to get into a poker game with every cent he had—ninety dollars. He lost it promptly, of course, to a gambler whom I later learned was named Tom Walker. Furthermore, Pete needed the money, and having lost it, whimpered some about it. There was no threat of fight, for Pete was as harmless as a kitten, but Walker—a bad one—hit Pete on the head with a beer bottle, and hurt the fellow badly. I had no idea who Walker was, of course, but when Crowe, the commissary man, told me the story it made me angry. Still, it was none of my affair, and I did nothing.

Not long thereafter, however, driving to the hotel from the camp one noon, I was hailed by the district attorney as I passed the courthouse. I've forgotten his name, but he lived at the Lake House, and I knew him.

I pulled up my team and he approached, putting one foot up on the side of the buckboard.

"Do you know a gambler named Tom Walker?" he asked.

"No," I replied, "but he nearly brained one of my men, and I haven't heard anything good about him."

"Well," he went on, "a man I know who would make a good witness in court, told me that he had heard Tom Walker say he'd get you."

I opened my eyes a bit wider. Walker evidently was a friend of Barns, for there could be no other reason for such enmity to me.

"Now, he's a *bad* man," went on the district attorney. "He's especially dangerous because he won't stand up and shoot you. He'll shoot from cover—" He nodded his head down the road toward camp "—from behind a boulder or a scrub cedar, when nobody's around. We're absolutely satisfied that he has killed two men, but we can't prove it."

"Hmph," I grunted. "What am I to do?"

"That's up to you. But remember that I've warned you. And don't forget to watch."

"Maybe I'd better go and kill him," I suggested.

"Well, if you do," he frowned, "come into the sheriff's office at once, and surrender."

"Yes," I objected, "and be locked up for a month. My business won't stand that."

"No," he insisted. "We won't keep you more than an hour or two."

I thanked him and drove off, a bit perturbed, you can be sure. I did not want to kill anyone, but I had no desire to be killed, either, and my mind was busy.

It had always been my custom, on leaving my team at the livery stable, to enter the hotel through the bar, that being the shortest route. I knew the bartender by now—a decent sort of fellow we called Barney—and went to see him.

"Barney," I asked, when I was sure no one else could hear, "does Tom Walker ever come in here?"

Barney nodded.

"Yes, sometimes," he replied.

"Well, point him out to me sometime, will you?" I asked.

"Glad to," he agreed.

"And don't say anything about my asking for him," I requested.

"No," he nodded. "I understand."

That Barney had more than a notion of what was up I do not doubt. Bartenders have a way of knowing things.

It was either that evening or the next—I forget which—that, coming in as usual through the bar, I saw Barney raise his brows at me. I went as casually to the bar as I could, and in an ordinary tone of voice, ordered a pony beer.

Barney drew it with his usual flourish and set it down before me, wiping the bar as he did so. The big room had not more than a dozen men in it, and none of them were near the bar. At the third billiard table behind me two men were playing, and farther back some others were at their ceaseless games of cards.

"Your man is sitting there at the end of the second billiard table, leaning up against the wall," Barney remarked very softly. "Don't look around yet."

I laughed.

"That's a good one, Barney," I remarked quite loudly, and drinking the beer—I do not like the stuff—I turned, and leaned my elbow on the bar, rolling a cigarette.

I glanced casually about the place and saw a man sitting in a splint-bottom chair, leaning back against the wall, and with his heels hooked over the chair rung.

I lit my cigarette and walked off to the lobby, where I took off my overcoat, and immediately went to my room.

I had learned in Idaho that the most effective way of covering a man without showing a gun was with a pair of Derringers in one's side pockets. Everyone knew, of course, that a man with his hands in the side pockets of a double-breasted coat had a Derringer in each hand. They are short weapons, single shot and hammerless, and so are perfectly adapted to such work, and I, already dressed in a corduroy suit with a double-breasted coat containing capacious side pockets, had a pair of Derringers in my room.

I got them at once, looked to see that they were loaded, and put them in my pockets. Down the stairs I went, and coming to the bar again, put my hands as carelessly as I could into those big side pockets. A glance from the lobby through the open door showed me that Walker was still where he had been, and walking into the bar, I spoke to Barney again, and turning about, headed along beside the billiard table toward where the men were playing cards farther to the rear. I did not glance at Walker, but as I came nearer I could see him out of the corner of my eye. I pretended to be walking past him, but when I was immediately before him I faced him and stopped, my bulging pockets plainly telling a man in his line of endeavor that he was covered.

"Is your name Walker?" I asked, and my voice was hard, I know, for I was tense.

I was looking him squarely in the eyes, and he was looking squarely back. He did not move, but I clearly saw the pupils of his eyes as they contracted. I had been told that the eyes of a frightened man did that, and now

I saw it happen. His pupils grew so small as definitely to change his dark eyes to grey.

"Yes, sir," he replied, and I particularly noted the "sir."

"Tom Walker?"

"Yes, sir."

"The district attorney tells me," I began, "that you've said you were going to get me, and that you're a bad man. He tells me that they're satisfied you've killed two men, but that you've done it from behind a boulder or a scrub cedar and they can't prove it on you. Now I don't want to kill you, but you're not going to kill me. I want you to leave this town and do it now. And don't you come back while I'm here. If you do, I have friends who'll let me know. The authorities will be on the watch, too. If you come back we'll find it out, and I'll shut down the work and send every man out to beat the brush for you. And when they locate you, *I'll* come, and when I come I'll come a-shootin' until you're dead."

Every soul in that barroom had dropped what he was doing. I had made no attempt to speak softly, and my voice must have carried clear to the lobby. There wasn't a sound when I had finished, but after an instant's hesitation Walker began to try to talk.

"Shut your mouth," I ordered, "and get out of here."

He made no effort to say anything more, but tilted his chair down and got to his feet. He turned toward the door leading to the street, and I kept facing toward him, my hands still on those Derringers in my pockets. It seemed to me that he made a little show of bravado as he crossed the room, but he did not pause, and walked into the street.

The men in the bar surged forward and crowded out the door, shouting after him.

"Leavin' town, Tom?" shouted one.

"Goodbye, Tom," bawled another, and they all laughed.

"He didn't get you that time," shouted someone else.

I went to the door presently and saw him as he reached the next corner and disappeared around it.

Barns and his partner, sobering up in jail, were finally released. But when they were they were escorted to the train and put on it.

Several years later I had some more work near Buena Vista, and going one day to get some supplies from "Doc" Wood, who kept a supply house specializing in supplies for ranches, I asked him if he remembered the incident of Tom Walker's leaving town.

"Sure," he replied, and laughed.

"How long did he stay away?" I asked.

"Oh," replied "Doc," "he's never been back since."

11

HAVING knocked Barns down had in itself brought me a little local celebrity, but following it up by sending Tom Walker out of town made, I suspect, a marked character of me. The business men of the town approved me for it, naturally, and my business was not hurt by it. Rather it was benefited, for what tough characters there may have been working for me felt more constrained to resist their wilder impulses. Among the gamblers and other toughs, however, I was far from popular, and many a time I noticed the animated buzz that so often went on in bars and gambling houses noticeably quiet down when I appeared. In such places I felt somewhat isolated, which hurt my feelings very little.

When I had come to Buena Vista the work that had been given me had not been very great. From time to time, however, more work was added and it was not until the following spring that I left. I did some work at Lathrop and in Trout Creek Cañon, enlarging the railroad yards in the town of Buena Vista itself, and finally, having obtained a big grading contract just outside Omaha, shipped my outfit east.

During my stay at Buena Vista, however, a man came to me and told me of two brothers, whose names

I have forgotten, who had staked out a mining claim not far away. He felt, so he said, that it was a good one, but the two brothers, in order to reach the deposit for which they were headed, had to tunnel for some distance into a mountain side. They had nothing, and were forced, periodically, to stop work on their tunnel in order to earn enough to "grubstake" them for a time. For that reason they had sent this friend of theirs to me.

If I, with my big outfit, would come and drive that tunnel in, and in addition would build a rough road for half a mile down to where the valley road ran to Lathrop, they would give me a one-third share in whatever profits their mine showed.

I was not especially interested, but finally agreed to look the place over, and in company with my informant, drove down. We left our horses a half mile or so from where the tunnel had been started, and meeting the brothers, started up the rough trail. We stopped at their cabin where they got some candles, and went on up the trail, with one of the brothers ahead.

We had not gone far when the leading brother pointed to the trail, upon which an animal's track lay in a soft place.

"Thet bar's been here agin," he commented simply, and went on.

But "thet bar's" footprints fascinated me. My experience with bears had been very limited indeed, but I knew enough to realize that that particular specimen was huge. His track, as I recall it now, seemed large enough for an elephant, and it was fresh, with the water still seeping into it from the side.

The brothers, however, did not seem unduly worried, and presently we reached the mouth of the tunnel.

Two men, working as they had been doing, had of course made the tunnel no larger than was necessary. One had to stoop a bit to enter it, and because I was their guest I was accorded the courtesy of going first. I ducked my head, therefore, and went in, walking slowly along the dim passage until the light grew very faint indeed.

I suppose that there was light enough for me to continue a little farther, but that bear track was in my mind. What if he had come in here? There wasn't room enough in that tunnel for him to pass us if he wanted out. If he was there, furthermore, he *would* want out when we came upon him. It appealed to me very little indeed, and I suggested that because I was not familiar with the place one of the brothers precede me with a lighted candle. Candles, however, cost money, and while one of them took the lead no candle was lighted.

We proceeded again, until we were a hundred feet or more from the dim spot of light that marked the entrance, when the leading brother stopped.

"You don't s'pose," he remarked, "thet durned bar's in here, do ye?"

"Don't know," drawled the other brother. "Might be."

We hesitated and talked a little, but finally went out. I don't remember why I did not accept their proposition. The task would have been easy and I had the men and tools. It would not have cost me more than a few hundred dollars, and I could have spared it. However, I turned it down, and forgot about the matter.

The sequel to this yarn came years later, after I had done many other things.

Having returned to Buena Vista at that time, I was standing in front of "Doc" Wood's store talking to him when I saw a snappy buggy pass. The team was smart, the running gear of the buggy was painted red, and in the seat, though the weather was not cold enough to warrant it, was a man dressed in a sealskin overcoat with a sealskin cap upon his head.

"Hmph," I grunted. "Another boss gambler's in town."

"No," "Doc" explained, "he's one of two brothers who have a mine not far from Lathrop."

"Brothers?" I demanded, and he told me the story.

No one had helped them out, but they had continued their hard work, finally reaching the ore. Then, not knowing what else to do, they mined it and sold the ore. They never organized a company, and having the money coming in they did not know what to do with it. They deposited it in the local bank until the banker would not take any more of it. The deposits of the two far exceeded all the money the owners of the bank possessed, and the brothers were finally convinced that they should bank the greater part of their money in Denver.

"What are they doing now?" I asked.

"Doc" pointed up the street to where a big house stood, a fountain playing in the front yard.

"The one you saw," he said, "lives there with an old maid sister."

"Where's the other one?"

"Oh," explained "Doc," "he's traveling in Europe."

And one third of all that money might have been mine! Those quiet, simple fellows would have been such perfect partners on a mine like that.

I had been to Omaha from time to time, and on one of my trips had had a talk with Bill Paxton, out of which the contract in Omaha developed.

Kansas City, always a rival town of Omaha, had developed as quite a meat-packing center, and some men in Omaha were determined to see what they could do. Bill Paxton was the leading, or one of the leading, spirits, and a company had been formed to start the work.

Three miles or so to the south of Omaha, therefore, they had bought a farm or two among the hills, and had decided to turn that hilly land into their meat-packing center.

Here was where I came in, for the hills must be graded down, the low spots filled, and eight or ten acres must be leveled off. It was quite a contract, but the yellow clay that lies along both sides of the Missouri River is perfect material to work.

My outfit was sent into camp upon this stockyards site, and work began. The Union Pacific, too, having decided to put a line in to connect with the stockyards, gave me that contract as well, and I was busy.

But now Omaha's emulation of Kansas City brought more work to me, although I had made no effort to get it.

Those who do not know the cities and towns along the Missouri often are surprised to learn that they are very hilly. That is especially true of Kansas City and only to a lesser extent of Omaha. But the hills one finds in those two cities today are only what are left.

Kansas City, in a fit of municipal energy, had gone to work and done a huge job of street grading, leaving buildings high above or far below the new street levels. Now Omaha, always with a jealous eye on the downstream city, caught the fever and drew up a tremendous program of street grading. The plans were drawn and bids were called for. I, however, busy with the stock-yards work, did not put in a bid, and was surprised when two men who had no outfit for such work came to me and told me that they had obtained a contract for a very considerable portion of it—the best work, in fact, that was let. They asked me, then, if I would do it for them, splitting the profits. I agreed, and before the month was out I had such an outfit working as would have frightened me two years before.

At the stockyards I was grading eight or ten hilly acres and grading for the railroad line as well. And now in Omaha I had to cut and fill I do not know how many thousand cubic yards of Farnam Street from Sixteenth Street to Fortieth, while I worked on Nineteenth Street and Twentieth Street as well. The Nineteenth Street job was the slightest of all this, and I let it to a sub-contractor, but Twentieth Street I kept, grading from Harney Street to Davenport, which required both cuts and fills.

How that yellow clay moved, and how, in the dry summer of 1884, the yellow clay blew! Few people in Omaha could fail to carry some of that dust home with them every night, and I, with twenty-two hundred men on my payroll, and with hundreds of horses, largely my own, at work, was a very busy person indeed.

In the midst of all this work the men on the stock-yards work struck. I was all for trying to settle the matter without an increase, for the margin I had was not wide. But Paxton and the others, coming after me when I was talking to the men, took me to the Millard Hotel where we had a conference.

"Get in here," Paxton ordered when he had driven his buggy out to the work and found me there. He was worked up because gossip had it that certain dangerous radical laborers from Pittsburgh, where they had been called "Molly Maguires" and had been credited with more than a few killings, had worked into the gang there at the stockyards.

"Get in here," he insisted when I demurred, telling him I had to talk with the men. "Damn it. Don't you know a lot o' these damn' "Molly Maguires" are here, and that they'll kill ye?"

I climbed in at that, and off we went to the hotel where I told them that I thought I could fight it out all right.

They, however, did not want the work stopped, and finally they asked me if one more cent a yard would be enough to satisfy the men. I figured awhile and told them I thought it would.

It did, too, and strangely enough that increase at the stockyards did not make me the slightest trouble among the huge gang I had on the street work in the city.

It was while all this work was going on that the campaign of 1884 was held, and I was asked if I wanted to run for the legislature again. I was nothing loath, but I was too busy to do much about it. However, I was nominated and re-elected, the January meeting of the legislature coming some time after the stockyards work had been completed, but very soon after the street grading had come to an end.

The stockyards company had erected, immediately after I finished my work there, the first packing house of what was later to become an enormous center, but they were having difficulty in convincing any meat packer to rent it. Later Armour, Swift, Cudahy, Sir Thomas Lipton, the Omaha Packing Company, and others built great structures there, but they did not appear interested at first. As a matter of fact, Paxton and his associates were able to get the first one to come only by giving them that new plant free of rent for a term of years.

Sometime during the late autumn of 1884, having been out in the state on some business or other, I was on the train coming back to Omaha, and coming on Paxton, I sat down with him.

"How's the stockyard coming on?" I asked presently.

"It ain't a-comin' very good," he replied slowly.

"I'm sorry to hear that," I went on. "You fellows have a lot of money in there——"

"Yes," he admitted, "we've got a bar'l of it in there."

"Well, what are you going to do?"

"Oh, by God," he replied, "we'll put in another bar'l. It's got to go."

I was impressed with his determination and his confidence, but did not realize that that little conversation would later help in preventing additional handicaps to the enterprise.

When the legislature met, my outfit was idle for the first time since I had started work nearly four years before, with the result that I had nothing to interfere with the session. Shortly after we arrived in Lincoln, Paxton came to me, obviously troubled and with a great handful of documents, asking my help.

There was in the legislature a considerable group of members who, as always, were opposed to almost any enterprise that centered in Omaha. This time it was the stockyard, which now was operating. What the details of the bill were I have forgotten, but it had been drawn up by a lot of short-sighted farmers who so often, it always seemed to me, were bent on interfering with their own best interests.

The superintendent of the stockyards, whose name was Babcock, was a member of the state Senate, and had done his best to defeat the bill, but he had somehow failed, and now the thing was due to come up in the House of which both Paxton and I were members.

All this Paxton told me now, and insisted that I take the papers he had brought and study them, in order the better to help defeat the measure.

I objected, telling him that he was the man to do it.

"Naw," he said, "I can't. Somebody'd start in askin' questions, and I'd get mad. *You* got to do it."

So I agreed, but I refused to take the papers. They were statements of investment and complicated tabulations of all sorts of things, I knew, and they would merely mix me up, just as they would mix up the minds of those whom we had to convince.

"No," I insisted, "I won't take them. If we can defeat the bill we can do it without that stuff."

When the bill came up, the House went into Committee of the Whole. The bill already had the prestige of having passed the Senate, and those who favored it stressed that point. Some amendment was proposed, however, and finally I got the floor. At some length I told of the value to the state of such an enterprise—of its value especially to the farmers. Then I told of the enormous labor that had been expended on it, and finally told of Paxton's remarks on the train, and especially of the "bar'l of money" that still had to go into it. Everyone knew Paxton, and knew his inimitable way of talking, which I did my best to imitate.

That story did as I hoped it would, and the bill was defeated.

It was at this session, too, that we had the task of electing a senator, legislatures not yet having been robbed of that responsibility. In the Republican caucus we had decided on John M. Thurston, but when the House and Senate met in joint session, we all knew that the first few ballots were for complimentary purposes, and that the real tug of war would come later.

This gave me an opportunity to pay a compliment to a Democrat whom I greatly admired—whom the country did, too, for that matter—and gave me an opportunity to tie a knot in the tail of an editor named Casper, who published a paper at David City.

J. Sterling Morton was the Democrat I so greatly admired. Less than two months later, Cleveland appointed him Secretary of Agriculture, and he is remembered now, of course, as the originator of Arbor Day.

The editor, Casper, had been a Democrat who, for some reason, had consistently opposed every move I had made. What the reason was I do not now remember, but I distinctly recall that I despised the man, though my reasons for that may not have been so sound as they seemed then. At any rate, from being a Democrat, Casper had swung around of late toward Populism, but with the election of Cleveland and the certainty that J. Sterling Morton would dispense the patronage in Nebraska, Casper began to try for the postmastership at David City. It was his obtaining this that I was determined to prevent if I could.

I had spoken to five Democrats, proposing that we give a complimentary vote to Morton for the senatorship, and they had promptly agreed. I was to propose him, and they were to vote for him on one of the early ballots. However, I now went to Casper and asked him to do the same, but Casper, as I had hoped he would, refused to support anyone whom I was for. Consequently, Morton obtained five Democratic votes and mine before, at last, the legislature chose Allen, defeating Thurston, whom we Republicans had favored.

I went, however, to see Morton as soon as I could after his six votes had been cast, and found him sitting in the lobby of the Lincoln Hotel. A man was standing before him and the two were talking when I approached, but he beckoned to me, and I sat down beside him. He was, I am certain, one of the most delightful and capable gentlemen I have ever known.

"Mr. Kyner," he said very simply, "I want to thank you for the compliment you have paid me."

I told him that I had been glad to have the opportunity, and before we finished our conversation I told him of Casper's having refused to join me.

"I want you to remember that," I remarked.

He smiled.

"Thank you," he replied. "I certainly shall."

When the new postmaster was appointed at David City I was very much pleased to learn that his name was not Casper.

As soon as the session was over I went to work to find a grading contract, and got one almost at once.

The Chicago, Burlington & Quincy had a branch line running north from their main line at Creston, Iowa, and this was being extended. The work was easy, and I obtained a part of it, which consisted of grading for a little track, of shifting the course of the Nodaway River, and of grading for the small railroad yards of a town that did not then exist but that now is known as Bridgewater.

Nothing occurred there that warrants recital, except for a typical display of honest Swedish conscience.

I had two Swedes working for me—brothers by the name of Anderson—and having dug the new channel for the little river, I gave these two the task of breaking through the last few feet of earth and of turning the stream. So confident was I of their integrity that I did not superintend the task, especially as I was busy elsewhere.

The two went off, and a day or so later returned, almost exhausted with their work.

"Finished?" I asked.

"Yas," drawled one of them.

"Did you do a good job?"

"Yas."

That was, I thought, all that needed to be said, but they still stood there, and after a moment I asked what they wanted.

"Mister Kyner," drawled one of them. Please don't send us to do like dat no more. Ve been 'fraid you t'ink ve not been vorkin', an' ve vork so hard ve all give out."

I wish more folks had consciences like that.

My work on the Burlington being completed, I went out to the end of the Fremont, Elkhorn & Missouri Valley—now a part of the Chicago & North Western—in order to get some work that they were doing on a continuation of the main line in western Nebraska, and on a branch that was to run north to Rapid City, South Dakota, from a junction point just west of Chadron.

C. P. Treat, who later became very much interested in the projected canal across Nicaragua which even yet has not been started, was the head contractor for the whole of that F., E. & M. V. work, and I found him at a headquarters he had set up at a place called Bordeaux. He showed me his profiles, and I got a contract for a mile of work very near the point at which the branch line to Rapid City was to turn off to the north, and having obtained it, hurried back to Omaha to get my outfit loaded.

Before I completed that first mile, I obtained additional contracts for other work, and though I did not know it as I hurried back to Omaha, I was to be engaged for some time in that desolate region. Treat, I learned later, did not expect ever to see me again when I left Bordeaux. The country was dry and rough and hard, and some contractors, having come for work, had not returned.

They, however, had probably not done any of that work on the Oregon Short Line which had served to harden me, while I, after Idaho, would almost have been willing to build railroads among the mountains of the moon.

I was back at end of track just as quickly as it was possible for me to get there, and pitched my first camp just beyond White River. Here I was again out in the wilds, with civilization off to the east of me, with the ranch country lying all about, with the roaring mining camps of the Black Hills not far off, in the land of freighters, cowmen, and bad men, but with my outfit busy.

12

IN THAT first camp on the F., E. & M. V. we were beside White River, at the very edge of the Bad Lands. We were to the west of the stream, and it interested me to see that the change in formation was so abrupt that the river seemed to be the dividing line between two sharply different geological formations.

Between Chadron, to which the track was laid within a week of our going into camp, and Rapid City, South Dakota, there was not a town, although the two must be all of ninety miles apart. Here and there along the way there were relay stations kept by the Northwestern Stage Company, and here or there a simple structure had been erected, but none of these attained the dignity of a town. Nor did a settlement need to be large to merit the name, either.

However, we were hardly more than six or seven miles from Chadron, and the question of supplies was simple. Treat, the head contractor, was building his office and supply stores there. Carpenters were busy building stores, saloons, gambling houses and a few simple dwellings, and the place had the animated atmosphere common to new towns just reached by railroads.

It did not take us long to complete the work on that first mile, and having obtained a second contract from Treat, we moved up the branch line that was to be built to Rapid City, and pitched camp again on the left bank of Horsehead Creek between two stations then nonexistent but now known as Siding Nine and Oelrichs.

Jonathan Crowe was still with me, in charge of the books and the commissary. He had several assistants, of course, but had become so much a part of my outfit that I would have felt lost without him. His wife, too, whom I have given scant credit, had been on the payroll as long as he had been, for though they had seven children, all of whom had lived for years in camps with us, she was responsible for feeding the men—a task that she handled better, I believe, than it was handled in any other construction camp I ever saw.

We were now forty miles or so from Chadron, and about fifty miles from Rapid City, in a desolate sort of country where few people lived.

Down the Horsehead a way a man had set up a saloon tent, and our commissary, of course, sold supplies to anyone who came, but there were not many people about, save on the road to Rapid City. A cowpuncher, however, from a near-by ranch, began hanging around camp, using the commissary tent as a loafing place, until all of us knew him. He was an amusing sort of fellow, who said little, and we came to call him "Doc" —though I doubt if I ever knew his name.

"Doc" had been in and out of camp many times when one day I saw him come in again all dressed up.

"Hello, 'Doc,' " I shouted at him as he approached. "What are you so dressed up about? Going to get married?"

"Naw," he replied, "I'm a-leavin' this country."

"Leaving?" I repeated. "Where are you bound for?"

"I'm a-goin' out t' Montany."

"What for?" I asked. "The railroad's coming in here. Things ought to be better before long."

"That's just the trouble," he explained. "I kin come in here and git a cigar for a nickel. I kin go down the crick a ways and git a bottle of beer for a quarter. That's too much fer me."

"Well, they'll cost you a lot more in Montana," I objected.

"Yes," he agreed. "That's jest it. I want t' go whar things is high."

He left, too, but I believe that he was the first man who ever suggested to me what has come to be so widely accepted now—that high prices and high wages go hand in hand.

This second contract of mine was a mile of fill, a simple task, with the work not heavy. It did not take us long, but I remember that while we were there Crowe's eldest son, Chester—a boy of eighteen—who had had tuberculosis for two years or more, grew perceptibly worse. He was a fine boy, who, earlier, had helped his father in the commissary, but who, because of his illness, had for months done nothing. The doctor had told them long before that he could not be cured, and the whole family, caring for him in every way they could, had grown to love him all the more because of his utter dependence on them. We all thought a great deal of Chet, but to his mother and his father he was a large part of the world.

Completing the work beside the Horsehead, we moved camp to the north another fifteen miles or so, to where a big cut had to be made, about two miles south of where the line was to cross the South Fork of the

Cheyenne River near the ford on the road to Rapid City. There was no town at the ford then, but the road was busy with wagon freighters and stagecoaches. The railroad was coming, and some saloonkeepers began at once to erect two places of business, while an unpainted, roughly built structure was thrown together to house three or four painted ladies such as were invariably to be found in the mining country and in every town where men from the railroad camps congregated. This cluster of three structures, one of which was as yet without a roof though the bar was installed, had no name, but it stood on the south bank of the Cheyenne, as we called the South Fork, and from a recent map I gather that it occupied the sight of the present town of Oral—a place I never heard of until I looked it up.

We were now working in a district that seemed to us to be one vast collection of fossil shellfish. Driving along the road, with the bright summer sun shining down upon the sparsely covered earth upon which the grass grew so thin as to make each blade seem to stand alone, I have seen literally millions of those fossil shells, turned by time and the dry air into all the colors of mother of pearl, and glinting with all the fiery vividness of a jeweler's case of gems. A hundred times, catching the flashing colors of rubies, of emeralds, of diamonds, off the road, I have pulled up my horses, and keeping my eyes upon the flashing light, have gone to it and picked up another fossil shell. I had a boxful of them at camp, into which I dropped the more interesting ones I found, and to which the men often brought the odder specimens that they picked up.

The cut we were to make was of considerable dimensions, and after getting into it our interest in fossils abated somewhat, for almost every yard we took from it and "wasted" on the dump was solidly made up of that endless mass of fossils.

We were well started on the work and I had been to Chadron two days earlier to get a little over three thousand dollars for my payroll, when an acquaintance of mine, Dr. Peter Schwenk by name, came through on the stage. Learning that he was bound for Rapid City, I told him that I was planning to drive up in a day or two, and asked him to stay and go with me. He assented and spent the night in camp, the stage rattling off toward the north without him.

The next day Chester Crowe died, and I have rarely seen such sorrow in my life. To have the boy they had grown to love so greatly die in a tent in that treeless, desolate waste of fossil shells was a terrible blow to that simple family. Nor was that all of it.

It was impossible to reach an undertaker. There was none within fifty miles. I am not certain that there was one that close. There was no minister, either. I thanked Heaven that Schwenk was there, and asked him if he would not be good enough to dress the boy and prepare him for burial. Schwenk consented at once, and went about his task.

But now the question of a coffin came to my mind. We could not purchase one, of course, save by sending for it, and days would elapse before it could possibly arrive. I looked about camp, but there was not a thing of which a coffin could be made. No trees grew near. There was no wood of any kind.

And then I thought of the carpenters I had seen at work there near the ford across the Cheyenne River. I spoke to Schwenk, and harnessing up a team, we started off to see if we could get two or three planks from which to build that coffin.

The ford was hardly more than two miles off, as I have said, but when we arrived and asked the owner of the half-built saloon if we could buy two planks or three, he told us that he could not spare them. It was not until then that we told him why we wanted them.

"Oh, help yourself," he told us. "Take what you need."

The carpenters, standing by, helped us choose the clearest planks, all of which had come rough-sawed from a sawmill farther north. And having pulled the planks out, the carpenters offered to build the coffin for us.

We thanked them, and they went to work, planing down both sides of those rough planks with the greatest and most sympathetic care.

A couple of the painted girls, sitting on the rough steps of the shack they occupied, overhearing the conversation, came nearer, and one of them, I remember, commented very gently upon the sorrow of the dead boy's mother. I had seen these painted women scores of times in the toughest, lowest places that could be found in the end-of-track towns all over the West, but I was about to learn a bit more of them.

They went back to their steps and sat there while those good-hearted carpenters planed and sawed and fitted. The coffin, within two or three hours, began to assume its shape, and the question of painting it came up. I thought a coat of black paint would be the thing to hide the glaring newness of that wood, but there was no paint of any color. And now one of those girls came up.

"Don't you think it would be nice," she asked, "to cover it with black cloth?"

We admitted that it would, but black cloth was not to be had either, as we told her.

"Well," she went on, "I have a black dress that might do."

And off she went to get it.

The dress, when she had brought it out, was black alpaca, and dresses being voluminous in those days, she and the carpenters finally decided that there was enough cloth for the purpose. She sat down, therefore, and with the greatest care cut the stitches and ultimately the work of covering the coffin began.

Another girl, who as yet had said very little, now asked if the inside should not be lined with white, and went immediately into their shack from which she brought a very pretty white dress that was not, I remember, of silk. But neither did it seem to be of cotton. Perhaps it was of wool.

"But that's your best dress," the first girl remarked.

"Yes," replied the other, "and I kinda hate to part with it."

I offered to buy it from her, but she shook her head.

"No," she said, "it's a pleasure to do it, and if I took any money for it I wouldn't feel that I had done anything."

My heart came into my throat a bit at that, and how distinctly I recall it. I put my hand on her shoulder.

"You're a good girl," I said, with my voice a little husky, and tears came to her eyes. I suspect no one had told her that for many a long day, and certainly I had never thought to make such a remark to any of those creatures of whom I had seen so many and held so low an opinion.

Those two girls helped to line the coffin. They made a little pillow for it. They counted the half a box of tacks one of the carpenters found in his toolbox, and having too few, the girls found pins to make up the difference.

Schwenk and I went back to camp before the task was finished, in order to send a wagon down to get the coffin. I saw it when it came to camp, and so perfectly had it been made that I feel sure that few would have noticed the difference between that hurriedly made, cloth-covered box and a coffin from some undertaker. There was a difference, however, for not a cent did the carpenters, the saloonkeeper, or those painted girls receive for their contribution to the funeral of that dead boy.

Chet was buried the next day among the million-year-old fossils of the hill near camp, and there he lies today. Neither Schwenk nor I ever told his broken-hearted parents where that coffin came from, and not until now have I ever breathed a word of it to anyone.

My trip to Rapid City with Dr. Schwenk had been delayed because of the funeral, but the day after it, we started off, with fifty miles to drive. We made good time, and must have been about halfway when, spying what was obviously a well-used camping place beside a little creek, I turned the horses toward it so that they could be watered, fed, and rested.

The stream was very small, but a little group of cottonwood trees stood there, their great grey trunks the more noticeable because of the rarity of trees, and while Schwenk took the horses off to a little pool a dozen yards away, I sat down on a big pile of rocks beneath one of the outstretched branches of a tall cottonwood, lit a cigarette, and began to open up the lunch that we had brought.

That freighters and travelers had long used the place as a camping spot was obvious. Scores of tin cans lay about, some long turned to rust. The remains of dead campfires were here and there, with stones about them, where pots and frying pans had been used.

As I was sitting there and Schwenk was putting the nosebags on the horses a six-horse team drove up, with two men on a freight wagon. I greeted them as they stopped, and knowing that so well-used a spot must have a name, I asked what it was.

"They call it 'Lame Johnny,' " one of them replied.

I laughed. Odd names are not uncommon in the West, but this seemed odder than usual.

"What did they name it that for?" I asked.

He climbed down from his wagon and came over toward where I was sitting on the pile of rocks.

"Well y' see," he began, "there used t' be a gang of horse rustlers 'round here, 'n' the boss rustler had one leg shorter'n th' other, so they called him 'Lame Johnny.' They ketched him finally up yonder toward the Gap, 'n' there not bein' no trees 'round there, they brought him down here 'n' hung him—" he pointed up to the big limb beneath which I was sitting "—on that limb. 'N' when he was dead they cut him down 'n' buried him right where you're a-sittin', 'n' piled some rocks over him t' keep the wolves 'n' coyotes from a-diggin' him out."

I looked down at the pile. It was eight or nine feet

long and five or six feet wide, and stood, I'm sure, fully three feet in height.

"Well," I said, "they put on plenty."

"Oh, no," he explained. "They didn't make the pile so big. But somehow, with the freighters a-stoppin' here 'n' all, they got to puttin' more stones on, 'n' now, when y' ask a fellow where he stopped, he'll say, 'Oh, I put a stone on "Lame Johnny." ' "

Schwenk and I ate our lunch, and when we came to go, I, too, picked up a stone and put it on "Lame Johnny."

We drove into Rapid City that evening, and went to the hotel at which the stage passengers always stopped. I am no longer certain of its name, but it seems to me that it was called the American House.

Both of us registered, and Schwenk having an errand, I sat down in the lobby to wait for him. I noticed as I sat down that a gentleman got up and went to look at the register. He then came over to where I was and, taking the chair next to me, asked me which of us was Mr. Kyner.

"That's my name," I replied.

"And is that your team of white horses that just drove up?" he asked.

I nodded.

He thereupon told me that several days before he had been on the stage from Chadron to Rapid City, and during the night the stage had stopped at the stage station on Horsehead Creek. This station was about fifteen miles or so south of where my camp was now located, and was on the road over which I had brought the payroll for my camp several days earlier. While the stage had been changing horses, my informant told me, the guards told the passengers of having caught one or two men whom they had seen hanging around not far from the station, under the impression that a new effort was being made to steal the relays of horses always kept at the station. Several times the horses had been taken, and the company had now hired two guards to keep rustlers off, the hostlers having been too easily intimidated. The guards had even gone so far as to put a rope around their captive's neck, preparatory to hanging him, when the fellow, insisting that he and his partner had not planned to steal the horses, told them that instead they had been planning to hold me up when I should pass with the payroll, for which they somehow knew that I had gone.

I thanked the gentleman for his information, assuring him that it was the first that I had heard about it, but that I would inquire at the stage station the next time I passed there.

I returned to camp a day or two later, but it was not until a week or more had passed that I had to go once more to Chadron, and so had an opportunity to learn something more.

A young cousin of mine, Jim Gunder by name, having recently been graduated as a civil engineer, had come to my camp to learn railroading "from the ground up" and had purchased two teams which we were using on the work. He was driving one, and had hired a man to drive the other, but the fellow had left some time before. But now Jim wanted to go with me to Chadron, so we started out, stopping at the stage station on the way.

The guards told us that they had let their captive go, convinced that the stage company's horses had not been the objective he and his escaped companion had had in mind, but that having seriously threatened to hang the fellow, he had peeled off his coat, his vest, and his boots, and then, with the rope about his neck, had told them every detail of the plans that had been laid to hold me up.

It had been their intention, so the guard told me, to take the money and my team of white horses as well, escaping across country in the buggy, leaving me to walk. That would have made it difficult for me, too, for my artificial leg had been bothering me, and I had, for that trip, left it in camp, taking with me a pair of crutches instead.

The man had been caught just before I, with the payroll, had driven past in the moonlight, and the guards had shouted to me, but the stage station was some distance from the road, and while I recalled having heard the shouting, I had not thought that it was meant for me. However, the fellow was gone now, and the guards did not know his name, while their description was vague and meant nothing to either Jim Gunder or me.

"But wait a minute," the guard went on. "When we took the rope off and he got dressed again he forgot his vest—kinda nervous I guess."

And off he went to get the vest, bringing it back from the stable tent where it was hanging.

"Well, what d' you know about that?" cried Jim when the vest appeared. "That's *my* vest."

A little more explanation told us that the man who had driven Jim's extra team of horses had borrowed the vest and had not returned it before his departure, and nothing more was needed to tell us who my prospective assailant had been. His first name was Bill, and that was all I knew about him except that he came from Pennsylvania, but I knew him well enough by sight.

We had wasted more than enough time about the matter, and so hurried on to Chadron, but the end of the affair was not yet.

Chadron was, of course, a very small place—gaunt, unpainted, and more than tough enough in spots. We drove into the main street, and as we approached the bank, I was hailed by "Shot Gun" Clark, the deputy sheriff. Clark had been for several years a guard on the stages carrying gold from the Black Hills, and had a reputation to be proud of in that country. He was a nervy little fellow, whose sawed-off shotgun had seen many a shipment of gold go through safely.

I pulled up by the board sidewalk, and as Jim got out to go about his business, Clark came up.

"There's a fellow here in town," he began, "who tried to hold you up out on the Horsehead. If you'll swear out a complaint, I'll arrest him."

"Oh, if he's here," I replied, "I'll 'tend to him myself."

Clark tossed up his hand.

"All right," he said, obviously willing to let me do entirely as I pleased.

I drove off toward the head contractor's office, and as I turned to cross a vacant lot, I saw before a cheap, unpainted, low-down saloon that stood in a row of such structures on the town's only cross street, no less a person than Bill himself. But my white horses were vivid in the late afternoon sunlight, and he saw me, as well.

I cut my horses with the whip, and turned down that street as Bill ran through the front door of one of those cheap saloons. I pulled up before it and leaped out, pulling my .44 as I went.

I yanked the door open and hurried in to see Bill as he reached the back door. He had it partly open when I shouted.

"Hold on there, Bill," I yelled. "I want you."

A man was banging a tinny piano as I entered, and a man and a woman were dancing. At a table a group were playing cards, and before the bar were a couple of men, talking over their drinks.

The piano suddenly ceased its noise. The dancing pair stopped where they were. Everyone stopped, and Bill, apparently with some notion of continuing his flight, looked back. I still had my gun up, and it was a potent argument, for Bill closed the door and stood there.

I walked over to him, half wanting to knock him down, but he was so obviously frightened that I could not.

"You damn' calf," I began. "I'd like to hit you, but I can't. Come here."

I forced him to the front door, and threw it open, stepping out behind him onto the board sidewalk.

"You see that road?" I demanded. "Well, that'll take you back to Pennsylvania. Now you get out of this country, for if I come across you again I'll take a shot at you."

He did not say a word, but obediently started off, while the people who had been in the saloon came pushing out onto the walk, shouting and laughing after the manner of their kind as they watched him go.

I left them there, with Bill still walking toward the east, and went to Treat's supply store.

At the camp we established while we cut through that great fossil deposit we bored a well, and after using the water for some time saw that our horses were losing their hair. We pondered and surmised and guessed about the cause, and finally were told that the water was responsible. It became necessary, therefore, to make a tank that could be put on a wagon, and in which we could bring water from the Cheyenne River.

I was told of a sawmill that stood up Fall River, a little way beyond Hot Springs, and so, with Higbee, one of my bosses, I went to get some lumber. We took a wagon, and Hot Springs lying almost exactly west of camp, we set out over a road we did not know, and forded the Cheyenne at a ford we had never seen before.

The distance was not great—fifteen miles or a little more, perhaps—and when, on the way, someone we met told us of a cave that had recently been discovered along the trail, we stopped and went in. There was a small opening in the rocks, through which a current of air blew with astonishing force, and though we poked about inside for quite awhile, we did not go far, for the single candle we had kept blowing out. Later the place became famous as Wind Cave, a very beautiful place and one of the many natural wonders of the Black Hills. At that time, however, it was almost unknown, and we had never heard of it until that day.

Having wasted a couple of hours there, we went on, and having obtained our lumber, started back for camp. Our sight seeing, however, had delayed us so that we did not reach the Cheyenne River until after dark.

The river was wide, the night was dark, and we did not recall whether the ford ran straight across the swift stream, or whether it angled upstream or down. Nor did we care to blunder in and risk driving into deep water, for that wagonload of lumber might drown the horses, even if we should be able to get out again. It was obviously necessary for one or the other of us to wade the stream ahead of the team, in order to find the way. On the ford we knew that the water was shallow—not much above the horses' knees, so going carefully there would be no danger. But oh, how cold the water of those streams can be!

My artificial leg gave me an excellent excuse for telling Higbee that he had to do the wading—an excuse of which I was very glad to take advantage. Higbee pulled off his trousers and his drawers, therefore, as well as his shoes and socks. But half a dozen steps brought him back. His bare feet could not stand the stones. Clad only in his shirt and undershirt, therefore, but with his shoes on this time, he started off, and waiting until he was well out in the stream, I drove the horses in. I could almost hear Higbee's teeth chatter above the rushing sound of water and the rattling of that load of lumber, and his shouted instructions came wavering back to me in a voice that seemed all hung with icicles. He was almost numb with cold by the time we reached the farther bank, and had had the additional misfortune of wetting a goodly portion of his shirttail. Furthermore, guided only by his shouts, I did not reach the farther bank until long after he did. He almost wailed as he urged me to hurry, and had not recovered his normal temperature even when we got to camp.

Our blacksmith built the water tank, and our water thenceforth came from the Cheyenne River, with the result that our horses quit losing their hair. I had learned, however, that one of my white horses had all the while been masquerading, for under his white coat his skin was uniformly black, which may be common enough among white horses, but I had never noticed such a thing before.

We finished our work among the fossils as autumn came, and having obtained an additional contract down on the main line, we moved our camp again, this time to the cañon of White River within a few miles of Fort Robinson, where the Ninth Cavalry was located.

The task I had ahead of me now presented some complications, for while the other contractors moved out as winter came on, I was determined to stay out there and work, thirty miles or so beyond the end of track, in a cañon that I knew might be cut off for weeks by blizzards and icy weather from the supplies and help that the railroad could bring only as far as Chadron.

13

THE CAMP we built at the head of White River Cañon was, I believe, the finest winter camp I ever saw. I had developed a good outfit, with many excellent men and a capable group of bosses, and I had no desire to let that force break up. Had I closed down for the winter, my men, of necessity, would have scattered all over the West, and I would have been faced in the spring with the slow and difficult task of gathering another force together. Fortunately, however, that was not necessary, for having gone over with Treat the profile of the projected work to the west, I had chosen a contract which both Treat and I felt was almost ideal for winter work if only I could store enough supplies to carry me through the period when blizzards and bad roads would keep the freighters from getting through.

I knew, however, that winter in northwestern Nebraska can be severe, and I decided that my first task was to create a camp in which all of us could be warm, comfortable, well-fed, and happy. Leaving the not quite finished work on the Cheyenne River, therefore, in the hands of Higbee and Bernard, both of whom, by now, had become my partners, but with interests far smaller than my own, I went out past Fort Robinson to the head of White River Cañon with a small force of men and equipment to build that camp.

The cañon is not long—not more, I should say, than two and a half miles—and our work lay at and just above its upper, or western end. On the south side of the river, which at that point is only a few inches deep and eight or ten feet wide, I found a perfect place for a camp. The work, it is true, was on the northern side, but the little stream created no problem. Instead it served as an excellent water supply.

Having worked for so long in the desolate, treeless region to the east and north, it was a pleasure to put up a camp where trees were so numerous. The cañon was filled with them, and on the level spot on the south bank where our camp was to be, the pines were plentiful, while the higher northern bank formed a perfect windbreak against the gales that blew so often in the winter from the north and west.

I had thought a good deal about how I wanted the camp laid out, and had sketched out a plan for a structure one hundred and seventy-seven feet long and twenty feet wide as the main building. This we built of logs, but in order to simplify the construction, we cut an eighteen-inch trench where the walls were to stand, and instead of laying the logs on their sides, stood them on end in the trench, shoveling and packing the earth in about their bases, and sawing the tops off even all along, holding them in position by heavy planks nailed firmly across the upper ends of the upright logs.

The structure ran approximately east and west, and while we cut doors and windows in the south side and a door in the east end, the west end and the entire north side were built without an opening of any kind.

The roof was made of saplings, on which we carefully piled a thick covering of pine boughs. Over these we put a thatch of coarse grass that grew along the river, and finally covered the whole with earth, until that roof stood a foot to eighteen inches thick.

In the west end, with double bunks built all around it, was the bunkhouse. The bunks were built in two tiers—an upper and a lower—and two men slept in each bunk. I forget how many men that place would hold, but with a great big government stove that I obtained at Fort Robinson, it was as warm and comfortable as a bunkhouse well could be, whatever the weather. Sometimes, in fact, when I went in, I wondered how the men could stand the heat.

Next came the blacksmith shop—not large, but very well equipped. Adjoining that were the quarters for the blacksmith, his wife, and little girl. The bookkeeper and his wife had their room next, and then came the commissary, with plenty of shelves, for the supplies would have to be stacked high in there.

The quarters for Higbee, Bernard, and me came next, with the dining room beyond, while the kitchen occupied the east end of that long, low structure, and lay within ten or twelve feet of the little river beside which, only a step or two from the kitchen door, we sank a box in the earth, and so built a kind of spring into which the water from the river seeped, giving us an excellent and plentiful supply of water.

The rooms were divided by board partitions, and every room, save the one my partners and I occupied, had an outside door. Ours, however, opened into the dining room on one side and the commissary on the other. On that account that one room had no stove, but all the others had, with a plentiful supply of wood at hand to keep us warm in any weather.

As a final precaution against the winter storms I set two men to work with a team and scraper, and they banked the long north side and the western end until the eaves were hardly two feet above the sloping protection of earth.

We built a stable too, of logs and brush and earth, and in Omaha I had an unusual stable tent made of heavy canvas—a tent in which the stall partitions and even the mangers were built of heavy canvas.

The eight thousand pounds of oats we ordered were in bags, and we stacked these carefully, stretching our old dining tent over the big pile. Extra commissary supplies, too, were stored in there, while tons and tons of baled hay were piled in the open. The winter's supply of food for the men made a huge pile, and what could not go into the commissary and the kitchen we stored in tents, for the time might come—was all but certain to come—when the roads would be impassable.

My wife, who periodically visited me in camp, was there while we were building the big log house, and while the work was going on she and I occupied a huge freight wagon box that I had had lifted from the running gear. It made a snug habitation, its canvas top proof against the weather.

A blizzard blew down on us the night before she was to leave for Omaha, and sweeping across the higher country to the north it drove enormous numbers of grouse and prairie chickens, jack rabbits, cottontails, and other prairie life into the protection of the cañon and of the spot we had chosen for our camp. We hardly felt the wind which swept high overhead but the fine light snow sifted down until our camp was buried in eighteen inches or so of the fluffy stuff. A wild cat—or what I took to be a wild cat—howled near by that night. I remember it because my wife was so obviously frightened at the sound, and the next morning the stormbound inhabitants of the prairie were thick in camp.

My wife and I started back to Chadron that day, for she was to take the train to Omaha, but on the road in the sheltered cañon the light and fluffy snow lay so deep that the horses waded belly-deep in it, and it pushed up so high before the dashboard that it fell over onto the buffalo robe that protected our feet. For over a mile—a mile and a half perhaps—the snow lay that deep, and the time we made was very slow indeed.

We stopped at Fort Robinson for the night, thinking to get an earlier start the next day, and found a very comfortable little log hotel just off the military reservation. The rooms in that log house had walls of boards, and the dining room walls were papered. The food and service were very good, too, despite the simplicity of the place.

There was another contractor—George Bell by name—in Chadron with his wife when we arrived. I liked George, except for one thing, which I had, in part at least, corrected. He had a team of driving mules that he bragged about to the point where it grew almost offensive. All of us, of course, swore by our horses, but George had always gone so much farther than the rest of us that I had begun to figure on how to take it out of him.

The opportunity had come several months earlier when, with our eyes on future contracts, he and I decided to drive from our camp out into Wyoming to where the line was ultimately to end, about where the town of Casper stands today. From Chadron to Casper is very close to two hundred miles, and I told Higbee, who was to accompany me, that I was going to show George's team up, for my team of white horses was, I felt, more than their match.

There is as much difference in the ability of men as drivers of horses as there is among the drivers of motor cars, and I was determined to prepare for that trip with all the care of which I was capable, and to drive with all the judgment that my thirty-five years with horses had taught me.

I went over their harness, therefore, and removed every strap that was not essential. I took off the hitching straps and checkreins. I fastened every flapping end, and turning my attention to the buckboard I was going to use, I cleaned it, tightened every bolt, took off the wheels and oiled them carefully with castor oil. I tied the oats, the mess box, the bedrolls and the water bucket tightly in place to keep them from shifting or from rattling, and altogether I made my preparations as if I were about to enter a race. What George did, I do not know, but his buckboard was identically the same as mine, and his supplies must have been about the same.

We started early, and as we were hitching up I recall repeating to Higbee an old verse my father had often quoted when he had begun to teach me about horses. It went as follows:

"Up the hill urge me not.
"Down the hill hurry me not,
"On the level spare me not.
"In the barn forget me not."

But that trip to the banks of the North Platte River, two hundred miles away, was very largely over level roads, and I had already decided to push my team in order to see what would happen to Bell and his mules. He was to take a foreman whom he called Pat, so the test was not likely to be unfair.

Out through White River Cañon we drove, and ultimately over the divide between White River and the Niobrara. It was after noon when we crossed the Wyoming line, and we camped that night near where the town of Lusk stands today. The next morning we started off again when the eastern sky was only half lighted by the dawn, and as dusk fell that evening we pulled up our teams on the banks of the North Platte River, directly across from the Goose Egg Ranch, at which the shuffling of the babies at the dance, as described by Owen Wister in *The Virginian*, actually took place.

We had come two hundred miles in two days, and having looked over the country carefully, laid our plans to start back early the following morning. Bell's mules, incidentally, had done very well, but more was to come, and I had not forgotten my purpose.

At dawn, consequently, we were off again, and about noon, as we were following the survey stakes across the prairie just outside the town that stood almost where Douglas stands today, with Higbee and me some distance in the lead, for Bell's mules were not so lively as they had been, it suddenly seemed as if the horses were trotting through shallow water. Such a thing out there on the prairie being so utterly impossible, both of us sat up suddenly and stared down at the horses' feet. There, without a doubt, the water lay two inches deep perhaps, but largely hidden among the prairie grass.

We had not recovered from that surprise when Higbee let out a shout and I pulled up the team as he leaped out. Turning about I saw him pick up a good-sized fish out of the grass. He picked up another and another, and I tossed him an empty bag to put them in. Bell and his foreman had come up by now, and Pat leaped out as well, adding to that collection of fish in the bag. They must have picked up forty or fifty pounds of fish before we called a halt, and driving on into Douglas we stopped at a little eating house where we traded that bag of fish for our meals.

We had, naturally, been mystified at first, but before we started off again we saw that a large irrigation ditch near by had broken, flooding that portion of the prairie and letting those fish go swimming about among the grass until the spreading water left them at our mercy.

We camped that night near Lusk again, and before dark on the fourth day we were back in camp once more. I unharnessed my team myself, and watched them carefully. They seemed in good shape, going out and rolling vigorously, and when, two days later, I had occasion to use them again, I found that that four-hundred-mile, four-day drive had not harmed them in the least.

Not so Bell, however. His mules had had too much. In fact they never got over the effects of that trip, and never again did he brag about that team, in my presence at least.

But now, with both his wife and mine in Chadron, he came to invite us to dinner. He had somehow managed to get a turkey, I remember, and it was served, but he also had a quart bottle of champagne—something I had never tasted. He poured a tumblerful for me, I remember, and when I tasted it, it seemed to be mild and much like cider. I tossed it off, consequently, without a thought, but then I found that it was less like cider than it had seemed. I recall getting back to the Depot Hotel where we were staying, but I slept all night without undressing, and woke up in the morning with a head that made me think that Bell had got back at me after all.

Chadron, by now, was growing to be a typical end-of-track town, and one of the structures that was erected was a saloon and gambling house which was the most complete and pretentious that I ever saw in such a place.

It was called the Gold Bar, and in lieu of any other sign it had the gilded likeness of a gold brick hanging above the door. The bar was large; the gambling room was most complete; and in addition it had a cross between an orchestra and a band that seemed never to stop for rest. The band held forth in a large room with a dance floor and with a stage for vaudeville performances.

Such a place was always well filled, of course, and often was crowded. On one occasion I was told that the man who was operating the Wheel of Fortune, and who answered to the name of Billy the Bear, had two artificial legs. I had already noticed that he had no fingers, barring a stump or two. We legless ones always seem to have a bond in common, so I went over to speak to him. The subject of artificial legs coming up, he asked me where I had mine made. I told him, of course, and he laughed.

"Why," he cried, "that's where mine come from. We must be brothers."

His name was William Yeager, and though I never heard his own account of how he came to be so maimed, I was told by others that he had been overtaken by a blizzard while he was on horseback. He remained on his horse until his feet began to freeze, and thinking to improve matters, he decided to try to walk for a time, leading his horse. Somehow, however, his horse got away, leaving him seven miles from the ranch house. His feet were frozen, and he could not walk, but he managed somehow to crawl that seven miles, with the result that his fingers froze, too, necessitating the amputation of fingers and feet as well.

I grew to know him well, and learned that operating a Wheel of Fortune in a gambling room was not a job that appealed to him in the slightest. He was doing it because he had not been able to get anything else to do.

"Is the wheel straight?" I asked him one day when we were talking together.

He looked about.

"No," he replied in a low voice. "There's not a square game in the house."

He did not stay there very long, and the next time I saw him was in Omaha, where he told me he was learning to use the typewriter. That was the last I ever saw of him, but I heard of him often enough, for he studied law and finally became the district judge in the very district where he had operated the Gold Bar's Wheel of Fortune.

On one occasion, having come to Chadron from the camp on White River, I was talking in the Gold Bar with "Cap" Smith of the Northwestern Cattle Company. The place was well filled, and as "Cap" and I were standing with our backs to the bar and our elbows on it, a cowpuncher came up with one of the girls of the place, stopping hardly three feet from us, where they stood arguing angrily with each other. The cowpuncher's back was turned to us when the argument reached its climax, and the half-drunk fellow suddenly slapped the girl in the face. She jumped back, of course, but "Cap" Smith, disgusted, as I was, with such actions, lifted his foot and caught the fellow in the back, shoving him so strenuously that he went staggering across the room until he brought up with a crash against the farther wall.

He recovered himself there, and pulling his gun he put a bullet through the ceiling and one into the floor with the most astounding speed. The men and women all about stampeded like a flushed covey of quail. They darted behind the bar and under the tables. They jumped behind the Wheel of Fortune and behind the doors. I was anxious to do a little stampeding myself, but "Cap" did not move, still leaning there against the bar, his elbows up behind him. The result was that I stuck it out, too, for I had no desire to show the white feather with him standing beside me, apparently so unperturbed.

The scurrying and the clatter of overturning chairs, however, had not yet ceased when "Cap" turned to me.

"Don't need to be afraid of him," he said dryly. "He's a good shot."

And he was right. The fellow put his revolver back into its holster, grinned sheepishly at "Cap," and went his way, while men and women reappeared from under tables and behind the bar to resume their former activities.

Our work in camp was progressing with the utmost smoothness. I wished that I had been able to take a larger contract, for it was very profitable, but when I had gone to Joe Millard, the cashier of the Omaha National Bank, and Wallace, who was, I believe, assistant cashier, asking them to go in with me in order that I might take more of it, they had refused. However, the contract I had taken was going perfectly, and I was very much pleased.

I had had, theretofore, no occasion to use carts on any work that I had done, but carts were useful on this work and I bought some. They were two-wheeled affairs, requiring but one horse for each of them, and had bodies that tilted when the catch that held them level was released.

A delightful Irishman had somehow come to camp —a man obviously superior to the other workmen. What his name was I have forgotten, but we called him Mike, and he was so good a hand with horses that I put him in charge of the cart work, telling him to pick his horses from the herd, and to put such men as he wanted on as cart boys. To my astonishment he said he did not want any cart boys, but being busy, I let him go ahead, and went off to Omaha on a business trip a day or so after the carts arrived.

When I returned after a week or so, I saw from a long way off that the carts were being used, and being interested, I drove up to watch. Certainly I was in for a surprise. Back and forth the carts were traveling, from the cut to the dump some distance off. They met and passed without the slightest trouble. They turned and backed in place where two groups of men were filling them, and once full went off to where the dump log lay which marked the edge of the dump beyond which the earth was poured. Here the carts were turned and backed against the dump log, but save for the men who loaded the carts and the man on the dump who released the catches, tripping the bodies and so unloading them, no one had a thing to do with the affair. Mike had, in that short time, trained those horses to go and come without a person at the reins or at the horses' heads, and only with an order now and then, or a push or pull upon the wheels to tell them how to back into some narrow place.

I was delighted, for Mike was saving me the wages of a man for each of those carts. And, too, cart boys could not have bettered the work that was being done. There was one trouble, however. The horses could not be made to work like that by anyone but Mike, and Mike had to have his fling occasionally. Many times I've gone looking for him among the saloons about Fort Robinson, bringing him back and letting him sleep it off. He seemed to know just as much when he was drunk as when he was sober, but he was not fit to work when his knees sent him staggering all about.

I grew tired of his drunkenness finally, and had a heart-to-heart talk with him. His breeding and his education had obviously been good, and I had learned that a younger brother was a successful small contractor.

As a matter of fact, the success of my talk lay in a joke that I played on him and not at all in what common sense I may have tried to impart. He was in his bunk when I went to talk with him, and I sat down upon a stool near by. It was cold outside and our big, warm log house had turned out to be a very desirable place to hundreds of field mice from the frozen prairie. They were always about, but no one ever bothered them and they had grown pretty tame as a consequence. And now, while I was talking to Mike, one of the little things ventured out onto the bunkhouse floor and sat up inquisitively not more than three or four feet from me, and even closer than that to Mike's bunk.

We both saw him, and Mike grinned.

"Look at that nervy little devil," he chuckled.

What got into me I do not know, but I looked blankly about as if I saw nothing.

"What are you driving at?" I asked.

"Why, that mouse," he replied, pointing to where the little thing was still sitting.

"There's no mouse there," I insisted.

Mike sat up.

"Do you mean to tell me," he demanded, "that there isn't a mouse right there?"

"Mike," I replied seriously, "if you don't stop drinking this lightning rod whiskey you'll be seeing elephants."

He dropped back onto his pillow and stared solemnly at the roof.

"Well I'll be damned," he muttered.

I almost laughed out loud, but managed to keep my face straight, and Mike evidently took my nonsense as gospel truth. Certainly he swore off drinking and was never drunk again as long as he worked for me. He stopped me one day, though, and wiping the back of his hand across his mouth, he said, "Mr. Kyner, I'd give a hundred dollars for a good big drink of whiskey—about a pint of it."

Fort Robinson, two or three miles away at the lower end of the cañon, was manned by a part of the Ninth Cavalry, which was made up of Negroes, and by a company of white infantry. We did not see much of the men, but one day, while a furious gale was sweeping across the prairie, a white infantryman and a colored cavalryman came driving into camp with a team and a light army wagon.

I was out on the work when they arrived, and returning, I entered the commissary to see the white man near the stove and the Negro behind the counter. I saw at a glance that both of them had been drinking, and asked the bookkeeper what the devil the Negro was doing in a place where we never allowed anyone but our clerks to be.

"I told him to keep out," the bookkeeper replied, "but he wouldn't."

I turned on him, therefore, and ordered him out of there. He threw his head back drunkenly and sneered at me.

"Come 'n' put me out," he replied.

The counter was between us, of course, and I could not reach him with my fist, so I picked up a light piece of stovewood from the box beside the stove, and reaching across the counter, brought it down with some little weight upon his head. He staggered back, and the bookkeeper dragged him out, with no objections being made by the fellow, either.

It was then that the white man, who was sober enough to see that they had made a bad beginning, told me that the two of them had been sent out to do some work on the army telegraph line that connected Fort Robinson with the army posts farther west. The gale was so bad, he said, that they had stopped, and now asked permission to spend the night.

I told them that it was quite all right for them to do so if they behaved themselves, and went off to wash up for supper.

Later, sitting in my room, I heard someone playing on the violin that the bookkeeper owned. That it was not the bookkeeper I knew instantly, for he could not draw a bow with such perfection. I listened for awhile, and wondering who the musician could be, opened the door that led from my room to the commissary and saw the white soldier with the violin beneath his chin.

Thinking it would add a little to the occasion, I picked up my guitar and entered just as he finished the piece he was playing, only to have him take the guitar, tune it, and play the instrument with such ability as to make me refuse to follow.

He entertained us with music so obviously beyond ordinary amateur standards that I commented on it.

"Why man," I said, "with a talent like that you ought to be on the stage. What are you doing in the army?"

"Yes," he replied, "I was on the stage, but I got to drinking and couldn't stop, and so I went into the army. It's the only place where I can stay reasonably sober."

They stayed all night in the bunkhouse, and when they left the next morning the white man asked me not to report them to the fort. I promised him I would not, and off they went—a blundering Negro cavalryman and that white soldier who, instead of repairing western Nebraska telegraph lines for the army, should so obviously never have been there at all.

We were as snug as we could be there in camp. Regardless of how cold it was, none of us ever felt it in that long log house, and when the men turned out for work they had to move about with some rapidity to keep from getting cold, which served, of course, to add to the profits of that job. During the winter the place was quiet enough, too, with little to take our attention from our work. During the autumn, however, I had seen a sight that seldom since those days has been seen in the West.

Major Andrews, the locating engineer of the F., E. & M. V., came to camp with a party of other engineers one day, and when they drove on to the west I drove with them for several miles. We had reached the higher land that lies between White River and the Niobrara, which there lies fifteen miles or so to the south of where our camp was, and could see a vast stretch of land up and down the Niobrara Valley.

We could see in the distance enormous numbers of dots, and when Andrews handed me his field glasses I made out plainly that the dots were deer, elk, and antelope. This was cow country, and I tried to see if any cattle were about, but I saw none, and handed the glasses back with some comment on the tremendous number of animals we could see.

Andrews, with the glasses, examined the distant herds with great care, obviously estimating their numbers, and when, having moved his glasses by steps from the western to the eastern horizon, he had seen all that could be seen, he dropped them.

"I would estimate," he said, "that there are about ten thousand animals out there—and there's not a cow among them."

I had seen a good deal of Western country before that, and saw more later, but never before or since have I seen game in such numbers as we saw that day.

We completed our work at the cañon in the spring, and got another contract farther west. I went to Chadron for the final settlement, and having obtained the check from the disbursing clerk, I took it to the Chadron bank on which it was drawn. When they asked me how I wanted it I told them I wanted currency. Had other contractors been at work I doubt if they could have paid it out, but as it was they did, though the bills were small, none being for more than twenty dollars.

I had a valise with me—a valise about eighteen inches long and ten inches wide, with a division down the center. When I put those stacks of bills in it, one half the thing was filled just even full. In the other half I put what I required for a quick trip to Omaha, and when I arrived there, I went at once to the Omaha National Bank, where Joe Millard, the cashier, and Wallace had refused to go in with me and make it possible to take a contract twice as large as the one I had just finished.

I asked for them, and when they appeared I asked them to take me into the board room. They did so, wondering, no doubt, what it was all about, but once there I put my valise on the table and opened it up, pointing to the piles of bills.

"This is what I've made," I explained, "on that White River job. If you fellows had gone in with me, the pile would have been twice as big."

"Hmph," grunted Wallace. "That isn't *making* money. That's finding it."

I think he did not give me quite credit enough, but I did not argue the point. I deposited that pile of bills to my credit instead.

14

WE MOVED from White River Cañon in the spring to a little piece of work ten miles or so east of Douglas. It was dirt work, with not a single pebble in it, and after the work we had been doing it was like child's play. Plows and scrapers did it all; the hauls were short and the earth piled high in every scraper. That soil almost seemed to be the answer to a railroad builder's prayer—if such men ever prayed.

The blacksmith I had had at White River had decided to return to Omaha in order that his little girl might go to school, but I found another excellent man almost immediately, and set him to work in the blacksmith tent far off at the other end of the new camp from the commissary and my quarters. I paid little attention to him after seeing that he was an efficient workman. He lived with his wife and three or four children in a covered wagon and a tent that stood detached from camp—beyond the blacksmith tent.

Shortly after we had settled down at the new work, a girl, trying to escape from a gambler at the saloon and dance hall ten miles or so away where she played her own low part, walked into camp and told her pitiful story to the blacksmith and the good-natured fellow's wife. They were gentle, generous people, and so pitiful did they find the girl's story that they took her in. I heard about it at second hand, and do not recall ever seeing the girl, for our force was large and I was busy.

A week or ten days after she had come, however, the gambler from whom the girl had run away somehow learned that she was in our camp, and with a companion came driving out, apparently to get her. I was out on the work when he arrived and saw neither him nor what occurred. Crowe, however, when I returned, told me that the gambler had demanded the girl of the blacksmith. The good-hearted fellow refused to give her up, and the gambler pulled a gun, whereupon the blacksmith grabbed a rifle and shot the fellow.

Such things were sufficiently common to create no great excitement, especially as the gambler had not been killed. To us the incident seemed to be closed, for the gambler's companion had bundled the wounded man into the buggy and taken him back to Douglas—or rather to the tent town called Antelope which lay just outside the townsite where Douglas came into existence a few months later. It was, we thought, a clear case of self-defense such as often had been allowed to pass without a word on the part of the sketchy law enforcement organization of the territory.

Two or three days later, however, a sheriff and a deputy or two appeared in camp with the announcement that the wounded gambler had died, and with a warrant for the arrest of our blacksmith. The poor fellow surrendered, of course, and off they took him—an example of law enforcement that created more talk and criticism among all of us in camp than the shooting had caused.

They tried the fellow, too—quite promptly—and, to our amazement, sentenced him to either one or two years—I forget which—in the penitentiary. It seemed to us that too many more shocking crimes had been committed without a move on the part of the law to make this seem like justice. Even the judge and jury must have thought the same or they would not have given the blacksmith so short a term.

What happened to the family I do not know. I only know that when that unfortunate wife left camp with her little flock of children, the girl who had unintentionally brought the trouble on went with them.

We completed that mile of work in thirty days, and as we were moving on to grade the railroad yards and the streets of Douglas, the bookkeeper gave me the final figures for the work. In that thirty days I personally had made almost three thousand dollars.

The town of Douglas, as I have said, had not yet been called into existence, but we had the task of building a part of the line close to the townsite, of grading for the good-sized railroad yards of this town that was to be a division point, and of grading the townsite streets. That the town was to be there everyone knew, but the railroad had refused permission for anyone to build within the limits of the site until the work was completed.

Just at the edge of the townsite, consequently, a temporary town had sprung up, housed entirely in tents. It was called Antelope, and was surprisingly complete. Groceries, dry goods shops, hardware stores were plentiful—all in tents. Flophouses and restaurants were similarly housed, and even a national bank, the name of which escapes me, displayed its name upon its canvas shelter. There were saloons and gambling houses in tents, as well, and a big dance hall was in full swing, its board floor covered by a tent.

The keepers of the livery and feed stable in the tent town, sensing what they thought was an opportunity, had gone about the valley before we arrived, and had taken options on every pound of hay. When I tried to buy some from them, consequently, the price they set was scandalously high, and I refused to pay it. Instead, I sent a wire ordering two carloads of baled hay, which could be had for six dollars a ton in Nebraska. The railroad freight cost me nothing, of course, though I had to pay the wagon freighters who brought what I required from the end of track fifty or sixty miles away.

The two carloads did not arrive, however, and I wired again. Somehow the second wire was taken as a second order for two cars, and four cars finally appeared —far more than I needed.

Shortly after it had been unloaded and stored at the end of track, Treat, the head contractor, came out on an inspection tour, and seeing all that hay, asked me what I was doing with so much. I told him the story, and he warned me that anyone from headquarters, finding me with so much that had been carried free by the railroad, might make a fuss about it, thinking that I was shipping hay at company expense in order to sell it at a profit.

"Then here's what I'll do," I replied. "Any contractor who brings me an order from you can get all he wants at exactly what it cost. Still, I can hardly refuse outright to sell it to anyone else, but I'll put a price of a dollar a bale on the rest. Folks won't exactly crowd in to buy it at that price."

He agreed and went about his business, and shortly after that the fellow from whom we were buying our drinking water and the water for our kitchen tent came up to get a couple of bales.

"How much do you want for it?" he asked.

"A dollar a bale," I replied with a perfectly straight face.

"A dollar a bale!" he bawled. "Why, it's Nebrasky hay, ain't it?"

"Yes," I nodded. "It's Nebraska hay. Cost me twenty-seven cents a bale at Chadron and the company delivered it free."

"Why that's highway robbery," he complained.

"Now listen," I insisted. "I'm buying water from you at twenty-five cents a pail—water that doesn't cost you anything."

He said no more. Rather than reduce his price on the barrels of water I was forced to buy each day he bought two bales at my exorbitant figure and hauled them off. Other sales at that price, however, were satisfactorily few.

The work at Douglas was reasonably extensive, but there beside the North Platte River the soil was light and the land was level. We finished up promptly enough, and with a fine profit to ourselves. For three years I had not touched a bit of work that had not paid, and much of it had paid me handsomely. And now we had another contract farther out the line, on Big Muddy Creek, to which we moved our outfit.

The work on the F., E. & M. V., however, was reaching its end, and leaving Higbee and Bernard in charge, I drove the ninety or one hundred miles to Fort Fred Steele on the main line of the Union Pacific, and leaving my team and buckboard there, took the train for Denver.

The Colorado Midland was being built, and I obtained a contract for two tunnels and some other work at the town of Manitou, some of the work actually lying within a few hundred yards of the Ruxton Hotel there. Going back to the Big Muddy camp, I told my partners what I had done, and they expressed some doubts about the tunnels, none of us having had any experience in such work. It did not worry me, but they fretted about it until they found a man whom they called Bill who, although I did not know him, had been in our employ for a little while. He said he was a tunnel man, and consequently, when we finally started the outfit for Colorado Springs, near which Manitou lies, it was with the understanding that Bill would be our tunnel boss.

Some time before I had purchased a very handsome and rather expensive bedroll of which I was inordinately proud. It had two beautiful California blankets and a buffalo robe that seemed as soft as silk. The canvas cover, too, was perfectly waterproof, and a pneumatic pillow added the final touch.

Going off ahead of the outfit, I put my bedroll, together with a lot of other equipment, in Bill's charge, and when I met the outfit in Colorado Springs I asked for my bedroll almost before I inquired about anything else. Bill told me that somehow it had been lost, but he seemed shifty-eyed about it. Where it had gone I could not tell, of course, but I know I felt positive that he had sold it somewhere along the way, and I ordered him to get out at once.

Both Higbee and Bernard were very much perturbed, and told me how much we would need the man.

"I won't have him about," I insisted.

"But the tunnels," put in Higbee.

"Are you fellows afraid to tackle them?" I asked, and when they admitted that they were worried over the prospect, I told them that I would attend to them myself.

We worked all through the autumn of 1886 and the winter that followed. The work on the first tunnel went smoothly and without a hitch. We bored through solid granite, and when it was completed the engineers accepted it without a change. The second one, however, was different. It was short, but no sooner had we started than we ran into what was called a "blowout"—a section filled with volcanic ash, with scoria, and quantities of plumbago, a kind of graphite that coated tool handles and the faces and hands of the men with a shiny black film that shone like polish on a stove. It was so slippery as well that we had to keep kegs of sand on hand, in order that the men could sand their hands and the handles of the tools they used.

The roof, too, kept falling in, and we had to timber very heavily, driving enormous quantities of cordwood "lagging" in above the timbers to keep that stuff from dropping down. At one end the top caved in so badly that we had to make an open cut of it, and when the tunnel finally stood completed, it was only about eighty feet in length. Years later even that came out, and an open cut was made of the whole thing.

There was, in addition to these tunnels, quite a lot of cut stone masonry to erect, for the road crossed a macadamized highway within the town of Manitou. This was new work for us, but we managed it, and in the spring moved to Buena Vista where, several years before,

I had done some work for the Denver, South Park, and Pacific.

We had spent the winter of 1886-87 in Manitou. My wife and boys had been with me in a cottage that I rented on the grounds of the Ruxton Hotel. The winter of 1887-88 we spent at Buena Vista working in part on a deep, solid rock cut.

All of this work had been profitable, and I was by now a man of more than ordinary wealth. How much I was worth I do not know, but I owned unmortgaged property in Omaha to the value of about two hundred and fifty thousand dollars, and that, together with my other investments and my outfit, brought the total close, I believe, to the half-million mark. When, in 1888, I obtained a contract for thirty miles of work on the Denver & Rio Grande, our outfit, in which I owned an interest greatly larger than did both Higbee and Bernard combined, employed twelve hundred men. How many horses, wagons, scrapers, carts—how many tools—how great a supply of equipment and supplies belonged to us I do not know, but it was very large. I distinctly recall that we were buying rutabagas by tons, powder by carloads, and that at least on one occasion I ordered a carload of dry salt meat.

The work that we had done near Buena Vista had proceeded well enough, the only major difficulty having been a premature explosion in which two men had been injured and another killed. As to profits, it had been entirely satisfactory, and now, from the D. & R. G., I had obtained a thirty-mile contract.

Between Glenwood Springs and Aspen forty-one miles of railroad was to be built. A firm by the name of Heckert & Day obtained the contract for the upper eleven miles, and we obtained the rest. Our outfit, too, had grown, and after we were well established on the work, of which we sublet the major part, our twelve hundred men were divided into three excellent, well-equipped, and very efficient camps, while at the very beginning of the work I deposited twenty thousand dollars in the then new bank in Glenwood Springs in order to meet our current expenses.

With so many men at work in the valley—how many the subcontractors had I do not know, but the total was large—it was only natural that saloon tents, gambling tents, and all the rest should drift in. It was not long until, from near Glenwood Springs almost to Aspen, the valley was dotted with them.

I did not set myself up as a monitor to guard the morals or the funds of the men who worked for us, but I was constantly troubled by the never-ceasing drunkenness, which disrupted our otherwise well-organized gangs. The work that we were on, too, was of the most difficult kind. A large cut turned out to be a constant struggle with a vast deposit of small boulders, ranging in diameter from a few inches to three feet or so.

We could not plow the stuff. We could not blast it. A scraper could not pick them up successfully, for even when a few got in, they rolled and jiggled out again before the dump was reached. Shovels were almost useless, and not a bit of our equipment served to handle the stuff. We finally sent our wagons in and filled them up by hand, the men picking the hopeless stuff up and loading it with nothing but their calloused hands to aid them.

Even the engineer admitted that he had no classification for it. It was far too large for gravel. It did not come under the heading of solid work. They had to call it loose rock, but ordinary loose rock could be handled far more readily.

But the drunkenness was causing trouble, and I had a talk with Heckert, the up-valley contractor, about it. He said that if I could get the tent saloons and gambling houses out he would stand one hundred dollars of the expense.

The job, however, was difficult. They were on government land, and they had government licenses. Had there been only one or two I would have attended to them myself. But in that forty-one miles there were dozens of them.

I was living at the Glenwood Hotel at the time, and while I was pondering this problem a newly arrived individual was pointed out to me. He was called "Doc" Halliday, and he had a reputation as a gunman that surpassed, I believe—in deadliness at any rate—that of any other person whom I ever happened to meet. It was told that he had been hired by a group of men who were trying to get control of a near-by coal deposit, and that "Doc's" task was to drive off the men who had staked claims there, in order that the whole deposit might be grabbed. Whether all that was true I do not know, but it gave me an idea.

He was living at the Glenwood, as I was, and was never to be seen without his partner, a man whose name I never heard. And it was in the lobby one evening that I spoke to him.

"My name's Kyner," I told him. "I want to have a little talk with you."

We went over to a seat well separated from the other people who were about, and I outlined my problem.

"Now what I want to know," I ended up, "is whether you can go up the line and drive those fellows out."

"Yes," he nodded, as if my suggestion was quite ordinarily businesslike, "I can do it."

"How much will you charge me for it?" I asked.

He did not hesitate more than a fraction of a second.

"Two hundred and fifty dollars," he replied.

"How long will it take you?"

"I can do it in a day."

"Well," I replied, "I'm living here at the hotel, and I'll pay you whenever you come in and tell me that they're gone."

What he did I did not see. I had gone quite far enough, and having hired him I kept away. One of my men, however, was in the saloon tent nearest our Glenwood camp. He told me afterwards that Halliday and his partner came riding up, and that "Doc" got off, leaving his partner outside. He came in quietly enough, but walked straight up to the man behind the bar.

"I want you to get this stuff out of here," he explained, "and leave this line."

The saloonkeeper patted the muzzle of a rifle that was standing there.

"See that?" he demanded. "I'm not a-goin' t' leave for you or any man."

"That's nonsense," "Doc" replied. "You take up that gun, and I'll bust it over your head. If you aren't gone when I get back, I'll move you."

He turned his back as if no gun stood there behind the bar, and walked out, getting on his horse and riding off. My man left, too, judging the tent to be a bit too warm, perhaps. But the next day, when I went down to look, the tent was gone, and though I never checked up I was told by several men that every saloon and gambling tent along that line had disappeared, save at a little village that stood in a draw a good half mile from the line.

I met Halliday the next evening in the hotel.

"What luck?" I asked.

"Oh," he replied, "they moved."

And without another word between us I paid him the two hundred and fifty dollars.

I never talked with him again, but coming into the hotel one evening rather late, I heard quite a buzz of revelry coming from the bar, which opened off the lobby.

"You're busy in there," I remarked to one of the owners who was behind the desk.

He reached down under the desk and pulled out a cartridge belt and a big revolver in a holster.

"Is that yours?" I asked.

"No," he explained, "It's 'Doc's.' He's gone in there to have a toot, and left his gun in here. Nobody'll shoot a man who isn't armed."

With so many men in our camps, minor injuries and illnesses were not uncommon. As a matter of fact, several major injuries occurred. We had to organize some sort of hospital service, and we assessed the men as a means of helping to carry the expense. But the work was scattered, and we required a doctor who would ride up and down the valley, taking care of the men. Furthermore, it was desirable that he be not only a physician, but something of a surgeon as well.

Having driven up to Aspen one day, I asked Heckert of Heckert & Day if he knew of such a man, or if he would try to locate one. He told me that he thought he might find one, and I went back down the valley hoping that he would.

A week or so later I drove up to Aspen again, and going to the hotel at which Heckert stayed, I asked for him. The clerk told me that he was in the bar, which opened from the hotel lobby, and I went to look for him. No sooner had I entered the bar than Heckert spied me, and shouted at me across the room.

"Hey, Kyner," he bawled, "I've got that man for ye. He's a cutter and a carver and a physicker too, and by God, he's one of our kind."

But he only thought he had him. The doctor, unknown to Heckert, was just outside the open door to the bar, and heard Heckert's announcement. His professional dignity was obviously hurt, for he appeared behind me at once and shouted angrily at my informant.

"Yes," he cried, "and you can go to Hell with your job."

He did not take it either, and I finally had to find my physician-surgeon in Glenwood Springs.

To add to our difficulties on the line from Glenwood Springs to Aspen we had to raise the wages of the men after we had accepted the contract. We had started out to pay a dollar and a half a day, but the Colorado Midland, which started some construction not far off, began paying two dollars. Our men naturally began drifting away at once and we had to meet that wage rate. It meant six hundred dollars a day to us, which was quite enough to take the profit out of our contract.

Still, the work was progressing and was, I think, two thirds or three quarters finished when I read in a railway trade journal that a railroad called the Lancaster and Hamden had been chartered to build a line in Ohio. The names of the officers were given, and knowing them, I instantly wrote, asking whether or not I might be given the contract for the entire line, some forty miles.

The answer I received was encouraging, and leaving Higbee and Bernard in charge in Colorado, I went east at once, and after much negotiation, obtained the contract.

Here at last was railroad work. I knew the country thoroughly, for the line actually went through Oakland, where I had lived as a boy. I knew the people. The work was not heavy, and gun-carrying bad men were unknown. What a relief that would be, and my wife and boys, with many friends and relatives about, could live in Lancaster where, for the most part, I could be as well.

Higbee and Bernard could complete that work in Colorado, and this little railroad would, I thought, set a perfect capstone on my fortune. Already I was a man of more than independent means—of wealth, as wealth was measured in the early nineties—of wealth even as wealth has come to be measured now.

This job, and I would retire. I thought that I had earned so great a luxury.

15

I WENT to work in Ohio with the rosiest expectations, only to find that there were many things about railroads that I did not know. I had been a contractor for some years and I knew the business, but the financing of such ventures was *terra incognita* to me. To me a contract had always been just a contract, and the officials of the roads for whom I had worked had had the responsibility of raising the funds with which to pay the contractors.

The Lancaster and Hamden, however, was being built at a time such as I had never before experienced. Without my knowing it, the depression of 1893 was on the way. Some stock in the line had been sold, and a bond issue was to be floated. From these two sources the expense of building was to be met. It looked perfectly satisfactory to me, especially as the estimates, for a little while, were satisfactory, and the payments for them were met promptly.

I was to do all the work, and things looked bright, but presently I was told that the money that had been raised by the sale of stock had been exhausted, while the bond issue had been delayed. I paid my men and bought my supplies, therefore, out of my own pocket. I could afford to, and thought but little of it. The following month the same thing happened, and the month after that. I was low on funds but had no trouble in borrowing what I needed.

Still, however, the bonds had not been sold. I plunged ahead, doing my work with all my strength. I borrowed more. But now the word that came from Higbee and Bernard in Colorado was bad. That thirty-mile contract was just about completed, but bills were coming due out there, and the payments did not cover them. I wired the two to raise what they could on the outfit that was there. They did and met the bills, but it took every item of that beautiful outfit, none of which I ever saw again.

I borrowed more and more, but property values were falling, and my holdings were soon mortgaged to the very hilt. I mortgaged the Ohio outfit, and being told that the bond issue still had not been floated, I myself went to New York to force it through. It was not until then that I realized just what had happened. Bond issues were impossible. Money could not be had.

I returned to Lancaster badly frightened. I pounded tables and argued. I fought and swore and fought again. But it was hopeless. I gathered up my last remaining assets—selling, mortgaging. I raised enough to pay my bills in Ohio. And finally, seeing at last the hopelessness of it all, I took a train for Omaha with barely money enough left in all the world to get me home. I could not even afford a Pullman berth. I did not buy a meal along the way, but existed instead on cheese and crackers that I had bought before I started.

There are, I do not doubt, many men today who have been through similar experiences. How much I had lost I do not know. I never had the hardihood to figure it out. I know that the two hundred and fifty thousand dollars worth of property I owned in Omaha, the value of which had of course fallen terribly, was mortgaged for every dollar I could get. My outfits in Colorado and in Ohio were gone. Every cent I had had was spent. All the securities I had owned and everything else that could be sold had long since gone.

I stepped onto the station platform in Omaha a tired, discouraged man. My wife had preceded me by a month or so, and when I reached home she put her arm about me and I cried.

What a tower of strength she was to me! For a time I could not bring myself to do a thing, thinking that the worst of calamities had befallen me—not knowing that what had happened was a trifle beside what was still to come.

I got about at last, trying to make a little money, but none was to be made. That year of 1893 had come, and with it every opportunity was lost.

I fought with every artifice I knew to keep my home. I traded horses when I could, but a year went past and what few dollars had been left had grown still fewer. At the stockyards in Omaha sheep were offered at fifty cents a head, with few buyers. Farmers were burning their corn because they could not sell it for enough to buy fuel. The whole nation was laboring under an economic collapse of such severity as to seem to us almost unbelievable.

Horses at the stockyards were selling at such ridiculous prices that even I could buy some. I bought a carload and took them east, selling them in Pennsylvania and doubling my money. Still it amounted to nothing, and a letter from my wife telling me that she was ill brought me home as fast as I could come.

The doctor's report was not encouraging, but I faced it as best I could. Her illness was extended—a serious operation was called for. She went to the hospital while holders of mortgages were hounding both of us. I fought them off—with nothing. I held them back in every way I could. To Hell with mortgages! How could I pay for the treatment my wife required?

A month passed. My wife grew weaker. The holders of those mortgages were constantly insistent. I fought with all my strength, my back against the wall. And now, on the thirtieth of March, 1895, my wife died.

I have no intention of attempting to describe the subsequent few weeks. I was left with two boys—one eighteen and one sixteen years of age. I had nothing. I owed the doctors, owed the undertaker, owed even for the cemetery plot where now my wife was lying.

That year was one of hopeless nonsuccess. I went with a railroad contractor to do some work in Wisconsin and took my boys along. I owned none of the outfit, and when the job was completed I had made nothing. I spent that winter in Omaha, fumbling at openings that did not exist, fighting constantly against the holders of those mortgages. I lost great sections of my property, staving off deficiency judgments by a hair. I was not myself, for I was fighting windmills constantly, or struggling with thin air.

What happened to me finally I do not know, but ultimately I quieted down. I somehow saw that I could not start again at the level from which I had fallen. I saw that I must start from the level I had reached. I could of course go to the devil, but that did not appeal to me, and anyway those boys of mine were my responsibility. They were enormous fellows—both over six feet already—husky, hardy, capable.

I thought of the Union Pacific Railroad where formerly I had had so many friends. But the U. P. had gone bankrupt, and my friends there were gone. Clark and Kimball could not help me now. Everyone I knew was gone—everyone but one old friend who, with his nose close down over his work, was holding on for dear life.

This one remaining friend in all the huge organization of the Union Pacific was P. J. Nichols, Division Superintendent of Division No. 1. It had been a long time since I had seen him, but time meant nothing to such a man as he. I went to him at once and told my story.

"Why, Jim," he said, "we're not doing anything."

I saw that he was thinking of new work—work for a contractor. I corrected him at once.

"Now listen," I insisted. "You've got a lot of people employed on the line. You know you can find something for me. I don't give a damn what it is."

He tilted his chair back and thought for a moment.

"Jim," he said presently, "the only thing I could give you is a job bossing an extra gang. But it pays only two sixty-five a day."

"All right," I replied. "What are they doing, and where are they?"

"They're bank widening," he replied, "and leveling the track a little. They're just this side of Central City now."

"I'll go," I nodded, "just as soon as I can straighten up some affairs in town."

"Well, when you get there," he went on, "you'll find one of my section bosses in charge. He'll tell you what to do and then he can go back to his section. Have you any horses?"

"P. J.," I replied quite seriously, "I haven't got a thing—not even a strap."

He told me a little more about the work, gave me a pass and a note to the section boss, and I left.

I do not believe that my two boys and I had so much as five dollars to our names. I had forty dollars a month which the government was now paying me for the loss of my leg, but aside from that there was not a cent. Yet Nichols had told me that a man with a team, working on that extra gang, would be paid three dollars a day, and I was determined to get a team. I somehow raised twenty-five dollars in cash. I have forgotten now how I did it, but I remember how fortunate I felt myself to be. Then, with a friend on my note, I went to Joe Millard at the Omaha National Bank and borrowed seventy-five dollars, having first found a team I wanted that was offered for one hundred. I remember how small I felt at borrowing seventy-five dollars from Joe Millard when only a few short years before I had shown him that valise half full of currency before I had deposited it.

However, I got the horses, and I bought on credit a forty-dollar set of harness. The Omaha Tent & Awning Company, too, sold me a twelve-dollar tent on time. How small that was when previously they had made tents to my order at prices up to six hundred dollars each!

And now, with those few purchases, I was ready. I

told my boys and they asked to go along. I told them that they would be paid only sixty-five cents a day, for such were wages in 1896. Still they insisted, while good old Pete Larsen, who had been hit on the head with a beer bottle by Tom Walker, the gambler of Buena Vista, and who through all of the past few years had hung around, even though I paid him nothing, went as well.

Our board would be supplied; we had a tent; we took some blankets from the beds at home, and off we went to Central City to work on an extra gang—a sort of peregrinating section gang of which I was to be the boss.

The gang was working not far out of town, pottering along at the work. With the four of us the total number in the gang reached fourteen, while only four or five teams were at work, even with mine added. How helpless and inefficient that outfit looked, scratching in the dirt beside the endless track, widening the banks, raising the track where it was low, lowering it where it lay higher than it should. There was, I knew, no other extra gang at work, and how endless the task appeared to me as I stared along the shiny rails that disappeared into the West.

But my luck was good, for Frank Schermerhorn, who was surveying and planting the stakes to show us what to do, came past that day. He stopped, and I talked with him about speeding up the force of men. He liked the idea, and said he would ask for it. His brother being the division engineer, I thought the order might come through, and within a few days it did. The force was doubled.

Tad and Gordon, my two sons, together with myself and my team, earned six dollars and thirty cents a day.

In addition to that I had my pension of forty dollars a month—a total of about $203.80 a month. How pitifully small it seemed, but how determined we all were to use every cent wisely! I owed one hundred and twenty-seven dollars in Omaha on the note at the bank and for the harness and the tent. We paid that on our first payday and carefully saved the rest.

For over two months we labored on the line, slowly working toward Grand Island. It was not easy, I can assure you. From seven in the morning until noon, from one o'clock to six, we worked hard. A man with an artificial leg does not find it easy to stride up and down a railroad track for ten hours a day and six days a week. Still, I did it, and never missed an hour. How I wanted to sit down, but there was no place to sit save on the polished rails. And when, finally, ten or eleven weeks later, we reached Grand Island, my boys and I had saved almost exactly four hundred dollars.

I bought another team of horses, consequently, and paid two hundred dollars for them. I ordered another set of harness from Omaha on time, and off we went to work again, our income increased by that new team. Now the three of us, and those two teams were earning, with my pension, about two hundred and sixty-five dollars a month.

Having a pass, I often went to Omaha on Sundays, for I was determined to get an outfit together again, and long experience had taught me that good secondhand equipment can often be purchased at a fraction of the cost of new stuff. I haunted the agricultural implement houses consequently, especially those that took equipment in on trade.

The first thing I bought in that way was a wagon—

a good one—for which I paid ten dollars. It was delivered to the freight station free, and the railroad shipped it to camp free. Later I bought more, but horses were my first concern.

We worked until sometime in December, reaching the little town of Wood River, a few miles west of Grand Island. Near Grand Island the work had been heavier, with the result that we could not move forward rapidly. But now cold weather had come, and the work had been suspended. We had been at work for seven months or so, and in that time had earned approximately fifteen hundred dollars. How few were the pennies we spent on ourselves, too! We were in overalls constantly—old overalls at that. We bought nothing for ourselves—literally nothing—forever looking for horses and equipment that we could afford to buy. And now, with the work suspended, we thought and planned and searched.

Prices for everything were still terribly low, but even with low prices we bought carefully. I bought four more horses at one hundred dollars a team. I ordered harness—good harness—paying up to fifty-six dollars a set for it. I ordered a good-sized stable tent in Omaha. I picked up several more secondhand wagons. I even had a wood and canvas bunk car made to fit one of the wagons, had it built sturdily and painted and so arranged that a group of men could lift it off and put it on the ground. It cost, I remember, twenty-five dollars, though surely the carpenter did not make much.

And now on one of my exploring trips to Omaha I found a prize—a prize that seemed at first to be a wreck, but which, having been repaired, did more than any other piece of machinery to put me back on my feet.

A patent grader called the New Era had been put on the market a few years before. I had never owned one, for they are not suited to rock work such as my outfits had largely been doing. But all this work along the main line of the U. P. in Nebraska was entirely dirt work. There was no gravel, even. For such a task one of these big graders was ideal. It plowed the dirt, and a conveyor belt took the dirt from the moldboard of the plow, delivering it some feet away out at the side.

It was one of those I found, abandoned in the weeds outside of Omaha a mile or two, its conveyor belt a rotten, battered strip of discolored canvas and one big wheel dished sideways. My first glance was almost enough to make me pass it by, but fortunately I looked more closely. It was rusty and looked as if it were hardly good enough for a junk pile, but a careful examination told me the contrary. A new belt, some repairs to that wheel, a four-horse evener and a pair of doubletrees was all it needed—all, that is, but grease and oil and adjustments.

I got a man with a team to haul it in to a wagon shop I knew, and left orders for them to repair the wheel and replace the belt. It cost about twenty-five dollars, I recall, which was little enough, considering that the machine cost twelve hundred, new. Once repaired, I had it shipped to Wood River, where we tinkered with it. We made a four-horse evener ourselves. We used a doubletree from a wagon. We oiled and greased and rubbed off rust. We tightened it and adjusted it, and in the meantime I was getting my outfit rounded out. Harriman by now had taken control of the U. P. The receivership had passed. Things, I knew, were about to happen.

When we had come to the end of our enforced two-month layoff, I was ready. I owned fourteen horses, twelve of which were required to operate that rejuvenated New Era grader. I had harness for them. I had a stable tent, a cook tent and a dining tent. I had four small sleeping tents and my own canvas and wood bunk car. I had bought a fine new steel cooking range for eighty dollars, and had spent another eighty on pots and pans, on enameled plates, cups, serving dishes, sugar bowls, et cetera. I had purchased knives and forks and spoons. I had two dining tables made, with tops and seats that lay upon collapsible frames that served for legs. I bought an expensive, all-steel plow, and paid forty dollars for it. A little collection of tools had been begun—a dozen shovels, a few mattocks, a little collection of carpenter and blacksmith tools, including a vise and an anvil. I had purchased a few scrapers at eight dollars each, and now, with all that equipment about once more, I began to feel a sense of power again.

For four years I had been almost penniless. From wealth I had pitched headlong to penury. And now I had an outfit once again—a small one, it is true, but a most carefully selected one. The tents were new. The equipment was, in large part, secondhand. Yet no one would have known it, so carefully had we repaired and cleaned and oiled and tightened. Our secondhand wagons rolled along with the solid sound of well-adjusted running gear. A trial of the big New Era grader made me tingle with pleasure at the sight. The horses were well fed. The harness was well kept and bright. The collars fitted. The horses were all soundly shod.

The world was round again, and I was in my place. It only remained for me to get a contract, and instead a contract came to me.

Dave and Henry Owen had been contractors on the F., E. & M. V. Their outfits put together had never equalled mine when I had worked on that line, but they were sound contractors and had gone through no such experience as mine. And now John Berry, formerly the chief engineer of the F., E. & M. V., was chief engineer of the Union Pacific. I had never known him, for all my work had been under Treat, the head contractor for the extension of the line. But the Owen brothers knew him well enough. Thus they obtained the contract for the bank-widening and track-leveling work which, the previous year, I had been doing as foreman of the extra gang.

But the Owens, fortunately for me, had never done any such work, and they wanted to sublet part of it. Henry Owen came to me consequently and offered me some miles of it at seven and one-half cents a yard. They were being paid nine or ten cents, but of course a subcontractor must take such work for less. I took it, consequently, and went to work at once, determined to work as I had never worked before.

For nearly a year my boys and I had lived as any section hands might live. And now, with a fine little outfit, and with a contract for which it was ideally fitted, the three of us went to Omaha in order to purchase supplies for our little commissary, and in order to celebrate. The celebration consisted of using some of the money that each of us had saved to purchase a new suit and a new overcoat and hat each, and of being seen in them by friends from whose lives we had disappeared for the better part of a year. Having thus recovered some of our confidence in ourselves, we took the train to Wood River and went to work.

How carefully I watched each movement of that little outfit! I asked the engineers how many yards of work lay in each hundred-foot section, for the work was marked precisely at every hundred feet. I studied every scraper as it moved, to see that it was loaded to capacity. I watched that big New Era grader, with Gordon at the reins, while Tad, his long arms busy, did the work always theretofore on such machines assigned to two men, handling the plow and elevator both, and piling up the dirt along the track in long, smooth windrows.

I figured on the backs of envelopes and in my note-book. I ordered the boys to grade down one side of the track and back along the other. Owen's grader, an identical machine, was using three men, and having graded down the track for a quarter of a mile or so, they turned out onto the prairie, and wasted the time of coming back. My New Era was moving dirt at less than three cents a yard. Theirs was doing identical work a few miles farther on for six. I was making as much profit at seven and one-half cents a yard as the Owens were making at more than nine.

I was on that job every minute. With about twenty men I was making an excellent return, and every dollar I was making was steadily going back into my outfit. After doing about twelve miles of work on the way to Kearney I bought on time another New Era grader—new this time, at twelve hundred dollars. I bought more horses. I redesigned my camping equipment. Moving camp was a frequent occurrence in those days, and I planned so as to eliminate every moment of delay. My bunk car on the wagon proved so handy that I had a cook car and a larger bunk car built. No time was lost now in taking down our tents and setting them up again. A few we had to have, of course, but I eliminated all I could. Stable and commissary tents and a few sleeping tents for men whose families were with them were still in use. But I trained the men to move them with almost Ringling Circus ease.

My credit, too, was good again—not large, perhaps, but good for what it was. I meant to keep it so, and realizing how far appearances carry one, I kept our camps more clean and orderly than any other camps I've ever seen outside the army. A Swede who had been a sailor worked for me as a general handy man. With sailor's palm and needle he kept our canvas perfect. I saw to it that no junk piles were about. There were no rusty tools, no broken equipment. Repairs were made at once. The stable tent was clean. The very arrangement of the camp was specified and orderly, each unit carefully in place in order to save work.

By the middle of the summer of 1897 I had twenty-nine horses where, a year before, I had had two. Old employees began to drift back to me. Crowe and his wife and children returned that summer, and others came as well. Things began to look as they had looked six years before, though never had I taken such care or watched details so carefully.

And when cold weather stopped the work at last, I was on my feet again. I had but little money, it is true, but I owned an outfit—an outfit, too, as large as that owned by the Owens brothers, with the additional advantage of containing two New Era graders while they owned only one.

I laid up my outfit that winter with some pride, you can be sure, and feeling free to do so, went east to rest.

The worst was over; I was on my way.

16

THE FIRST summer as a subcontractor with the Owens had re-established me, and for four years I continued on that work. I did work at or near Sydney, Julesburg, Chappel, Kimball, Pine Bluff, and elsewhere. I even straightened out the tangled mess of my affairs in Omaha, recovering practically none of it, it is true, but escaping from deficiency judgments and other such difficulties—even realizing a little, from time to time, on my equities.

My boys and I had reached an equitable arrangement, and once more I was the sole owner of an excellent outfit, different in character from the Owens' outfit, but more competent as well. They were equipped only for dirt work. I could work in dirt and rock as well.

My old acquaintances, Kilpatrick Brothers and Collins, had obtained a large contract for some heavy work between Cheyenne and Hanna, in Wyoming, and the Owens, somewhat overreaching themselves, took a contract for a very large and difficult rock cut in Wyoming, only a few hundred yards west of Tunnel No. 1 on the main line of the Union Pacific, near Walcott. But having obtained it, the task began to assume proportions in Hank Owen's mind that troubled him. He had never done any rock work, and his outfit was not fitted for it.

This cut, however, was nine hundred and fifty feet long, was to be put through solid rock to a depth of eighty-two feet. A total considerably in excess of one hundred thousand cubic yards had to be moved, and that is quite a bit of rock anywhere, while this particular cut lay in a land where water was not at hand, where winter was coming on, where supplies must all come from points up to six hundred miles and more away.

It is not surprising that a man who had never tackled such a task should hesitate. I had taken my first comparable job in large part because I was inexperienced and did not know the difficulties. Owen knew enough to see the difficulties, and turned the work over to me, not as a subcontractor, except technically, for he did not get a penny from it.

I had by now made myself ready for such work and I took the contract with some pleasure. Here was the largest single rock cut I had ever tackled. I was to learn that it was the most troublesome and difficult as well. But the fact that it was winter work did not bother me. In this dry country nothing but our drinking water would find it possible to freeze. Certainly the rock could not—or could not freeze, at any rate, to the damage of the work. The only trouble lay in the short days, but the railroad was anxious to complete the work as soon as possible, and I determined to work day and night.

We began the erection of camp in the autumn of 1900, and realizing that comfort was essential if I were to make rapid progress, I tried to think of everything. Every man that could be used was to be put to work, and having gone over the ground carefully, I reached the conclusion that three hundred men was about the limit. To go beyond that was merely to clutter up the place to no purpose. As it turned out, the force fluctuated from about two hundred and sixty, at the smallest, to about three hundred and twenty-five at the largest during the ten or eleven months we stayed there.

The first things we erected were two water tanks which, together, held five thousand gallons. That solved the water problem, for the railroad had tank cars with which to supply their needs at certain of the towns along the way, and these tank cars brought our water as well. The tanks stood just beside the track while the camp lay down a slope below. The arrangement was ideal, for three hundred feet of pipe took the water down to the kitchen and the watering troughs, while in the kitchen a coil in the stove and a tank gave the cooks and dishwashers a plentiful supply of hot water.

The kitchen had a dining room on each side of it, with every care taken to insure convenience. These were built of wood and canvas, but the two bunkhouses, the commissary structure, and the powder magazine were built solidly of wood. The horses were stabled under canvas. Three canvas and wood bunk cars were in use, and in the structure occupied in part by the commissary was my office and the office of the camp doctor, while the upstairs was assigned to the foreman of the outfit.

I had married again the year before, and my wife and I were housed very comfortably indeed in one of those wood and canvas cars built to be carried on a wagon, but now firmly established on the ground.

That outfit was the largest I had ever had in one camp, and the camp was, I suspect, the most efficient and complete of any I had ever had. In Colorado we had had far more men on our payroll, but they were scattered among three main camps and several smaller ones, while the time that had elapsed had seen improvements made in tools and equipment. Four years before, I had had to borrow three fourths of the money necessary to buy one hundred-dollar team. Now I was established in a big camp, with everything at hand that I required, and I owned every bit of it save a steam shovel outfit to which I sublet some of the work at the western end of the big cut. That outfit, with its fourteen men and two teams, was the only part of all that collection of equipment, of structures, of supplies, that did not belong to me, and aside from current bills, none of which were large, it stood free and clear of every cent of debt. My credit was excellent; I had enough cash to carry on the work, and while I bought with very great care, there was nothing that I needed that I did not purchase. Each double bunk, for instance, had four blankets—six hundred in all—and they were mine, while everything else was done as completely and as well as care and common sense dictated.

We worked two ten-hour shifts—the larger one working during the day—and tried to arrange our blasting so as to have the shots fired in the morning and evening while the men were off the work. It was not always possible, of course, but we tried for that, and saved time and expense by doing so.

The west end of the cut was an almost vertical drop. Throughout the great mid-section the depth was reasonably uniform—eighty-two feet—while at the eastern end it slid off more gradually and yet was too steep for horses until we had moved a lot of surface earth and rock in wheelbarrows.

The rock moved by the steam shovel was taken away

in dump cars on a track. Elsewhere, wagons and carts were used throughout the work, the first step in which was to blast out a twenty-foot "lift" throughout the length of the big cut, wasting it over the sides among and upon the stunted sagebrush.

I came into the commissary one day, and was told that one of the foremen had sent a man up to get his time. It was not an unusual occurrence, and I would have thought little of it had it not been that through the window I saw the fellow trudging off with a blanket under his arm.

In such a camp, filled with men of every sort, one has need to watch out for his property. More than enough of it is bound to disappear, and this departing man, as I could see quite plainly, had a blanket rolled up under his arm—a brown blanket.

Now those six hundred blankets that I had in camp had not been bought for nothing, and here, I thought, was a man walking off in broad daylight with one of them under his arm. I determined to get my property and bring it back. I did not have my gun on, and did not think of getting it.

The man had walked around the work, curving back beyond it to reach the railroad track. I was able, consequently, by taking a more direct path, to come out on the railroad not far behind him in a little rock cut just out of sight of camp. The drills, the steam shovel, and the other noises of the work came plainly to our ears; but though we were not far away, we were out of sight, and no shout could possibly have carried to camp above the noise of the work.

I thought nothing of that at the time, but shouted to the man who was still forty or fifty feet ahead. He stopped and turned around as I came up.

"What do you mean," I began, "by carrying off one of my blankets?"

He tried to tell me that it was his own—that he had brought it with him when he came. The rolled up blanket was brown, however, as all the camp blankets were, and I would not listen to him.

"You can't tell me that," I shouted. "I supply the blankets in this camp, and all of the ones in the bunk-houses belong to me. Hand it over here."

He didn't argue much, which convinced me the more that I was right, and presently he unrolled the blanket, took out a shirt that was his only other possession, handing the blanket over to me. He turned and walked off when he had handed the blanket over, leaving me to carry it back to camp.

I had not told anyone what I was going to do when I had left the commissary, but sometime after I had returned, the timekeeper asked me where the blanket that I had thrown on the counter had come from.

"From that fellow that got fired," I explained shortly. "He was carrying it off."

The timekeeper picked it up and examined it.

"This isn't a camp blanket," he remarked. "It belonged to him. I remember that he had it when he came."

I felt pretty badly about that. The fellow may have been all sorts of an undesirable person, but a blanket and a shirt had been all that he was carrying. Now I had taken his blanket from him. I did not understand why he had not objected more strenuously. Nor did I understand any better when my elder son came to me.

"Pop," he began, "you shouldn't do a thing like that. That fellow was a bad man. He always had a gun, even when he was out there on the work. He could have killed you, and none of us would have known about it for hours."

Other men about camp—though whether they knew what they were talking about I do not know—said that the fellow was a renegade. If that were the case, it seems strange that I had been able to rob him of his blanket quite so easily.

Now and again we had to fire "shots" while the men were on the work. Firing sixty or more kegs of powder at a time, as we did, gave the earth quite a jolt and sent the rocks hurtling all about, of course. But it almost seemed to me that the men sometimes went fully halfway to Ogden each time the warning came, and spent whole hours of time wandering back to work when the rocks had ceased flying. I was, consequently, always trying to set them an example, and usually stayed well within the range of flying rock, staring up and sidestepping the stuff as it came down.

On one occasion, doing as I made it a habit of doing, I bawled at them for going so far away and stayed in close myself. The "shot" went off; the air was filled with flying fragments of rock, and I was staring up in order that I might keep out from under any that came my way. One piece, however, came whirring along a flat trajectory, and hit me a blow on the knee that hurt like fury. How I wanted to sit down and rub that painful spot! But the men were all about, and I felt I dared not do it. Instead I hurried them back over the bank into the cut, and not until every one was out of sight did I sit down and rub that spot. I stood a wee bit farther off after that.

The powder magazine of such a camp is not a place to which just anyone is given access. As a matter of fact, only one man in that camp—a foreman—had the key to the place.

I was looking about for him on the work one day, and not locating him, I headed for the magazine which stood off by itself at some distance from the other structures and from the work itself. The weather was cold by now, and the dynamite, of which we had only about a thousand pounds, was apt to freeze. A round, coal-burning cast-iron stove, therefore, had been installed in the middle of the magazine floor, and a fire was kept burning there to keep the dynamite in usable shape. Even with the stove in the place, however, the sticks were often too hard to use, and so it became the custom to stand the sticks that were to be used on end about the stove, leaning them against the ash pit, in order to thaw them before taking them out for use.

I reached the magazine and tried the door. It was unlocked and I went in, only to stop in my tracks, unable to decide what next to do. There lay the foreman, drunk and fast asleep upon the sanded floor just beyond the stove. The stove, too, had one side cherry red, while about the base and within a foot of that red-hot spot, eighteen or twenty sticks of dynamite were standing.

Should that fellow turn over and brush against those sticks, an explosion might result. A dynamite salesman, only a short time before, had tried to demonstrate how safe his explosive was. It would not explode, he explained, save with a cap affixed. And to prove his point he threw two inches of a stick against a near-by rock. It went off with a flash of white light and a blast that almost floored us, and this dynamite about the stove, I knew, was even less safe than the salesman's explosive had been. And too, if one of those sticks went off, every particle of the thousand pounds or so would follow. The foreman and the magazine would be no more than a memory, and even that might have a hole or two blown in it.

I stepped out quietly and got another foreman. Together we sneaked back and gathered up that dynamite, putting it aside most carefully before arousing the sleeping fellow and taking him to his quarters. I did not fire him either, for without exception he was the best man in camp. He *would* get drunk now and then, it's true. But never again did he do so inane and dangerous a thing.

With so large a gang at work among the rock, it was certain that there would be injuries from time to time. I consequently looked about for a camp doctor, and finally got Dr. Schwenk to come. He was the same person who had been with me when Chester Crowe had died, but I have done scant justice to him, and have not attempted to describe him at all.

I am not a tall man myself, at that time standing a trifle over five feet nine. My sons, however, were taller —Tallmadge, whom we called Tad, being six feet four and Gordon reaching six feet two. Dr. Schwenk, however, was inches taller than either of my boys, and while I am not certain, it seems to me that he stood a little more than six feet six inches in his shoes. Furthermore, he was ideal for the work that devolved upon him. He could be gentle, as had been proved to my satisfaction when Chester Crowe had died, and I have seen him when he could be something else.

I had equipped an office and an apothecary shop for him, and had placed it next to my private office. Only a board partition divided the two rooms, and I could plainly hear what went on in there.

On one occasion an excitable fellow with a cut on his wrist appeared at Schwenk's office. The cut was not bad, but as the doctor treated it the fellow squirmed, whimpered, and grunted until Schwenk grew angry. I heard him as he tried to soothe the fellow, but when that didn't work, he shouted at him suddenly.

"Shut up, damn you," he roared, "or I'll box your ears."

Not another whimper came to my ears during the remainder of that visit.

Schwenk and my two sons were with me one evening in the commissary when Barney Sullivan—himself six feet tall and Irish as well—came in and told me of four gamblers who had got their names on the time book. They had been in camp for some days, but had worked only enough to be permitted to stay, and played cards every evening. With their sharpster tricks they were, of course, taking money away from the men, in addition to keeping other men in the bunkhouse awake.

"They're over there now," explained Barney.

"Then I'll just go over," I replied, "and tell them to get out."

"Better not try to do it alone," objected Tad.

"Bosh," I replied, and started out.

Tad, however, insisted on following me, and Gordon followed as well. Dr. Schwenk, too, not to be left out of it, trailed along also, and Barney Sullivan's Irish blood made it impossible for him to stay behind.

So there I went, a poor enough likeness of Frederick the Great, no doubt, but with a squad of men such as might well have come from his regiment of giants. Schwenk, as a matter of fact, was a descendant of a member of that very regiment, and would have been an exceptional man even in the regiment to which his ancestor had belonged. It is no wonder that the group of poker players about the bunkhouse stove looked up as I entered with the four biggest men in camp at my back.

"You fellows get out of here and get out now," I ordered.

One of them tried to argue the point, showing me some clothes that were drying on a string above the stove. Another wanted to stay all night and leave in the morning.

I would not listen. I pulled the clothes down and dropped them on the fellow, ordering them off at once. They said no more, but silently got their belongings together, walking through the door in a group. I followed, with my giants at my heels, and shouted after the fellows as they strode off through the starlit night.

"Keep going," I ordered. "If you change your minds and come back here, you'll find somebody waiting for you."

We had removed about sixty of the eighty-two feet in the big cut, and were working on the last "lift" when

I went over to where the three holes for a new "shot" had been drilled. Dynamite had already been set off at the bottoms of the holes, "springing" them and creating openings in which the black powder was being loaded. Three such holes, on that job, constituted a "shot," and in each of those holes we usually put twenty kegs of powder—sixty kegs, or fifteen hundred pounds of powder in a single explosion. Such a blast is, as you can see, something more than a firecracker.

The first hole had been successfully loaded, but the second had had only eleven kegs of powder poured in when a stone, somehow dislodged, plugged the drill hole leading down through twenty feet of rock to where the dynamite had "sprung" the opening. The powder man had tried to dislodge the stone with a loading stick but had failed, and having wasted quite a bit of time, the foreman, an excellent man, had gone to the blacksmith shop for a long piece of round iron rod. As I approached he had the rod down the hole, and was trying to drive it through with a striking hammer.

"You ought not do that," I warned. "We had an explosion in Buena Vista and killed a man in just such a fool way."

"Well," he explained, "I can't force it out with the loading stick. What else can we do?"

That the thing was dangerous I knew. I had rolled a cigarette, and it being contrary to the rules to light a cigarette so near a loaded hole, I turned about to walk off a way in order to light up and think it over. As I turned, the loader came up to the foreman.

"Let me have the hammer," he remarked.

"No," objected the foreman, "this is dangerous."

"Well, it's no more dangerous for me than it is for you," the loader insisted.

I did not see or hear him hit the rod, but I was told afterward that he struck it only once. What I did see was a crack that opened suddenly beneath my feet—a crack in which I saw a flash of fire. Then my back buckled as I have had it buckle in a very rapid elevator that starts too suddenly, but vastly more exaggerated. I felt myself going up.

I had often read of how many things go through one's mind at such a time, and now I experienced it. I recall thinking of an acrobat I had seen, who had dived off a springboard, and in mid-air had turned a somersault and landed on his feet. I wondered if I were going up and then were going to turn over and come down, rocketlike, upon my head.

And then, quite suddenly, I struck. I do not remember that it hurt so much. My breath was knocked out of me, and I presently began to struggle to get it back. Before that, however, I had heard the foreman's voice, and had felt him pull my cigarette holder out of my mouth. Then I heard the voice of the Hungarian boss of a Hungarian group we had on the job, and managed to get breath enough to ask how the loader was.

"He's not suffering any," the Hungarian replied.

And presently, with my wife running excitedly over the broken rock fragments, a group of men came hurrying with a cot on which they carried me to our quarters. The doctor went over me with the utmost care. My back was strained and bothered me some, and one of the small bones in my ankle had been slightly fractured. That bothered me a good deal. But it was two or three days later that I got the worst jolt. It was only then that I was told that the loader had been instantly killed.

It was about that time, too, that the Hungarian boss, with a group of his men, appeared at my quarters. I could see them as my wife opened the door, the whole group standing there with their hats off. They had come to ask how I was, and to return my cigarette holder. They had found it among the broken rock where the foreman had tossed it when, thinking I was dead, he took it from my mouth.

I was interested, naturally enough, to learn how far the explosion had hoisted me into the air, and Harry Neal, a nephew of mine who was working in the commissary, told me that he had been looking in my direction when I went up. At the side of the cut, fifteen feet above where I had been standing, a rock stuck out in the crude likeness of a face. The men in camp had come to call it "the old man," and Harry told me that I went up just about that high, which, I can assure anyone, is quite high enough if gunpowder happens to be the propelling agent.

We finished that cut in just a little less than a year. The railroad company had been fearful that I would not complete it by the time they required it, and in their efforts to expedite the work had made a big dirt fill at the western end that should have been made by material from the cut. Because of this and other reasons, I had a large claim for damages. The claim never came to trial, for the company offered to settle it, and I accepted. But even without that I made good money. Incidentally, to the railroad men and the people of that country 'round about, that big cut is still known—though quite unofficially—as Kyner's Cut.

The explosion, however, had frightened my wife. She urged me to quit railroading. The idea, too, was not distasteful to me. I had lost a fortune more than comfortably large, and now, within five years, had built myself a competence again. Perhaps I'd better quit.

I had rented a New Era grader and eight horses to the Owens, who had taken a contract in Iowa. The rest of the outfit I disposed of in Wyoming, and having received an offer from the Owens for the purchase of my eight horses and the grader, I went to Omaha to settle up the matter.

I met them in their room at the Murray Hotel, and promptly learned, to my amazement, that though they had had my horses and my machine for months, and owed me a round sum for their use, they now proposed to wipe that debt away, merely dating back the purchase of horses and grader to the time when they had rented them.

I objected.

They insisted.

I rose from my chair and went to the door. I turned the key in the lock and taking it out dropped it into my pocket. It was their room, of course. It was not a matter for guns, either, for none of us had guns. But I was determined.

"Now, damn it," I told them, "you're going to settle with me, and you're going to settle my way."

They did, too—promptly—paying me what I felt was justly due, peeling it from a roll of bills that they had earned, in part, by the use of the horses and the grader they were buying.

For two or three years I pottered about the West, but I accomplished nothing. And finally, going east with my wife and very young daughter, I bought an old colonial home just outside the District of Columbia, within six miles of the White House. The old house appealed to me in part, perhaps, because the date high up one of its tall chimneys is 1746, which antedates my own arrival in this world by just one hundred years.

Here, with seven acres of garden and orchard and lawn to interest me, I have stood aside for the past thirty years and let the world go by. Busying myself with bees and dogs, with chickens and with a horse or two, modernizing and reconstructing this old, old house of mine, I have played no part that could be felt so very far beyond the pillars at my gate.

I have seen, as from a seat in a theater, the drama of the world. Here and there it touches me, of course, but mostly it does not.

The World War came, as war came over seventy years ago when I was very young. It passed, as the Civil War passed, though with less of wounds and death and poverty to those of us in the United States.

An expansive era followed, not so vastly different from that earlier era of expansiveness in which I made a fortune for myself. A depression followed that, as a depression had followed before. Fortunes were lost, as mine and many others were lost in 1893.

People are again fearful of the future, as many of us were fearful in 1894 and 1895. I have talked with many people of the problems of today, and the burden of their queries always seems to be "What lies ahead?"

Why, opportunity lies ahead, of course, as it did in 1893, for those who would work for it. But then, it isn't everyone who can look at periods of depression from the vantage point of eighty-nine years, as I can.

I can so plainly see the struggles of the nation, trying by a greater complication of government to create an easier life for the people. I can only shake my head, of course, and no one listens to me. Yet I feel reasonably certain of my opinion. No people ever prospered by being protected from life. It is the struggle that makes them strong. It is the struggle, too, that is the reward in life. Pampered peoples cannot possibly be strong. I watch with some distrust the growing complication of government and law. I look with disapproval on vast new edifices being erected by the government to house vast numbers of new bureaucrats and departmented dependents who perform duties all too unimportant for the costs they bring. This growing complexity of everything does not improve us. I wish for simpler things, myself—simpler things in government, in business, in society, in life.

I have played my little part, for good or ill, and now am merely waiting. So much of what I've seen and done is distant and like a dream, that it was with a shock that, seventy years after I lay there on the bloody ground, I visited the battlefield of Shiloh and stood before the tombs of men whom I had known there.

How strange a thing is time! How strange a thing is memory! And yet the strangest thing of all is the restless urge that forever lies within a man.

The end of track, I realize, is not far off for me. And yet I've often seen the very best of contracts lying at the end. It may be that my track will end that way. I hope it will. I like to feel that I am ready still—for anything.

Notes

No attempt has been made to provide a complete annotation of Kyner's memoirs. The purpose of these notes is to amplify references in the text to certain persons, places, and events which might perhaps be confusing, or on which the reader might desire additional information.

Page 80, line 16

The "Colonel Mathewson" referred to is probably Charles P. Mathewson, a prominent resident of Norfolk, Nebraska, and agent for the Winnebago Indians. His title derives from service as lieutenant colonel of the 11th Connecticut Volunteers in the Civil War. See J. Sterling Morton and Albert Watkins, *Illustrated History of Nebraska* (Lincoln, 1904, *et seq.*), II, 325-326.

Page 85, line 21

Kyner is mistaken in assuming that this hunt of the Poncas was the last to occur in Nebraska. The Pawnees were on a buffalo hunt when they were massacred by the Sioux in southwestern Nebraska in 1873. Buffalo-hunting was common until 1875. See Mari Sandoz, *The Buffalo Hunters* (New York, 1954).

Page 93, line 29

Thomas L. Kimball (1831-1899) later became vice president and general manager of the Union Pacific. Kimball County, Nebraska, and Kimball, the county seat, were named for him. Notes on Kimball's activities will be found in Thomas M. Davis, "Lines West!—the Story of George W. Holdrege," *Nebraska History,* XXXI (June, 1950), 108-110, (September, 1950), 212.

Page 94, line 1

Casper E. Yost was publisher of the *Omaha Daily Republican,* and later became president of the Northwestern Bell Telephone Company. See *Northwestern Bell,* XXXIV (June, 1954), 14; Morton and Watkins, *op. cit.,* I, 493-494.

Page 94, lines 3-6

A biographical sketch of P. W. Hitchcock (1831-1881) will be found in Morton and Watkins, *op. cit.,* I, 495. Gilbert M. Hitchcock (1859-1934) is treated at length in Robert F. Patterson, "Gilbert M. Hitchcock, A Story of Two Careers," unpublished doctoral dissertation, University of Colorado, 1940.

Page 94, line 29

The Commercial Hotel was located at 11th and P streets in Lincoln. For a note on its role in Nebraska's politics, see James C. Olson, *J. Sterling Morton* (Lincoln, 1942), p. 279.

Page 95, line 3

Senator John M. Thurston (1847-1916) was long a powerful force in Nebraska politics. Thurston County was named in his honor. There is no definitive biography of Senator Thurston, but considerable information on his career can be gleaned from Morton and Watkins, *op. cit.,* and Addison E. Sheldon, *Nebraska: The Land and the People* (Chicago, 1930). See also *Who Was Who in America* (Chicago, 1942), I, 1238.

Page 96, line 10

Bill Paxton was William A. Paxton (1837-1907), a prominent Omaha merchant. See Morton and Watkins, *op. cit.,* I, 731-732.

Page 111, line 15

Kyner has misspelled the first name of Sidney Dillon. A sketch of Dillon will be found in *Dictionary of American Biography,* V, 312.

Page 125, lines 24-29

For a colorful account of the notorious Olive gang, and particularly of the career of I. P. Olive, see Mari Sandoz, *The Cattlemen* (New York, 1958), pp. 186-204.

Page 136, line 21

Kyner probably is referring to Silas Henry H. Clark (1836-1900), general freight agent and later president of the Union Pacific Railroad. See Morton and Watkins, *op. cit.,* II, 603-605.

Page 150, lines 5-6

Kilpatrick Brothers and Collins were among the largest of the railroad builders in the West. The partnership consisted of the four Kilpatrick brothers of Beatrice, Nebraska, and C. W. Collins of Brooklyn, New York. See Morton and Watkins, *op. cit.,* I, 599-603.

Pages 192-193

J. Sterling Morton's attitude toward the senatorial contest to which Kyner refers is discussed in Olson, *op. cit.,* pp. 350-351.

Page 251, lines 20-21

Joseph H. Millard (1836-1922) was a pioneer resident of Nebraska territory, a prominent banker in Omaha, and United States Senator from Nebraska, 1901-1907. See Morton and Watkins, *op. cit.,* II, 305-306.